FACTS

FACTS

by

George H. Kendal

BUTTERWORTHS Toronto

Facts
© 1980 Butterworth & Co. (Canada) Ltd.
All rights reserved. No part of this publication may be reproduced, stored in a retrieval system, or transmitted, in any form or by any means, photocopying, electronic, mechanical, recording, or otherwise, without the prior written permission of the copyright holder.

Printed and bound in Canada

The Butterworth Group of Companies
Canada:
Butterworth & Co. (Canada) Ltd., Toronto
Butterworth & Co. (Western Canada) Ltd., Vancouver
United Kingdom:
Butterworth & Co. (Publishers) Ltd., London, Borough Green
Australia:
Butterworths Pty. Ltd., Sydney, Melbourne, Brisbane, Perth, Norwood
New Zealand:
Butterworths of New Zealand Ltd., Wellington
South Africa:
Butterworth & Co. (South Africa) Ltd., Durban
United States:
Butterworth (Publishers) Inc., Boston
Butterworth (Legal Publishers) Inc., Seattle
Butterworth & Co. Ltd., Ann Arbor
Mason Publishing Company, St. Paul

Canadian Cataloguing in Publication Data
Kendal, G.H., 1907-
    Facts
    Includes index.
    ISBN 0-409-84245-1

    1. Evidence, Expert — Canada. 2. Law and fact — Canada. I. Title.
    KE8472.K46   347.71′067   C80-094266-3

For Sophie

Preface

The simplest factual probe will follow some rules, even if they are not made explicit, and formal rules of procedure and evidence may allow latitude in application. Procedural rules govern the manner and form in which expert evidence is given. This evidence is decisive where technology assessments and scientific evaluations are needed. Impersonal as this evidence is, it is liable to affect the lives and fortunes of many.

Rules on expert evidence have recently undergone considerable changes. The most far-reaching of these gives Federal courts the power to call, on their own, expert witnessess to clarify, supplement or contradict the evidence of experts called by either party. Some ordinary courts of the land have followed suit. This power is not entirely new. Until, some generations ago, it fell into disuse, it was considered to be an inherent part of the power of Common Law courts with general jurisdiction.

The revival of this discretionary power constitutes a radical departure. To turn it into actual practice, it is not enough to give an account of ostensive shortcomings of the old rule and of immediate advantages of the new. The basic premises, and wider consequences of this change will have to be scrutinized. Only if this is done, can sufficient criteria become available for a decision whether the present reluctance to exercise this discretionary power is justified. This decision will affect not only court proceedings; the practice in hearings of commissions of inquiry, administrative boards and other public fact-finding bodies, while largely free of formal rules of procedure and evidence, will here be influenced by the example set by the courts.

The hallmark of modern proceedings, in common law and many civil law jurisdictions alike, is that in litigation the initiative of adducing evidence lies wholly with the litigants. Hence the new rule on expert evidence introduces a triadic configuration into a frame of rules designed to hold adversary polarities. This arrival of a strange element in surroundings, which have for long been taken for granted, provides alternative viewpoints. The mere presence of the new rule among familiar rules points to new perspectives on the problems of fact finding in general and, in particular, on technological and scientific issues. To test the trustworthiness of these perspectives, the primary conditions, which make a finding of fact possible, will have to be re-examined. The results will then be related to those adjustments of the fact-finding task which ongoing accelerations of the rate of change demand.

Table of Contents

Preface vii

CHAPTER 1 FACT FINDING 1
The Search for Evidence 1
Description of Change 2
The Seriation of Perceiving and Remembering 2
The Historicity of Behaviour 6

CHAPTER 2 SYSTEMS AND TOPICS 9
Technological Behaviour 9
Familiarity 10
Sweeping Change 11
Problem Solving 12
Order 14

CHAPTER 3 SCRUTINIZING 17
Wholes and Parts 17
Quantification and Meaning 17
Probability and Truth 18
Relevance 22
Describing 25
Contradicting 31

CHAPTER 4 SUPERSTRUCTURES 43
Interpenetrations of Public and Private Law Elements 43
Machine-regulated Behaviour 55

CHAPTER 5 PROCEDURE AND EVIDENCE 65
Atomic Facts 65
Pleadings 73
Evidence 77
Trying the Case 80
Metaphysics of Facts 84
Shifting the Burden of Proof 88
The Adversary Principle 91

CHAPTER 6 A CONCLUSION 97

Appendix A: Gorgias on What is Not or on Nature 101

Tables: Axioms 30
        Profiles 47
        Rule-Changes 76
Index 105

We have an incapacity of proof, insurmountable by all dogmatism. We have an idea of truth, invincible to all scepticism.

Pascal, Pensées, 395

Chapter 1

Fact Finding

THE SEARCH FOR EVIDENCE

Evidence establishes a matter as a matter of fact. The evidence of the conditions in which one form of matter can be transformed into another was the starting point of the search for the simple structure elements of the world. Each structural level that was reached pointed to a deeper one. For a time the simplest elements were supposed to exist at the sub-microscopical level. In probing this hypothesis a regression was encountered in which matter performed a vanishing act. In a current view, matter is no more than waves of probabilities travelling through a non-medium of multi-dimensional non-space. The black holes of astronomy, a discipline from which modern mechanics developed, are a mathematical formula rather than a hypothesis of physics. Moreover, the recourse to negative description brings an encounter with the antinomies of negation. These reappear in logic as its self-reflexive paradoxes. Again, the evidence of fundamental regularities which physics seeks has not been obtained by putting energy into the place of matter. This principle remains in the realm of abstract notions, and even there the dynamic character of irreversible changes can resist mathematical formulation. The path of modern science which began with the refusal to save appearances is leading to a refusal to save meanings.

Yet, in terms of the human world, this situation holds promise. The promise springs from the renewed appreciation that the distinction between behaviour directed towards the things in the world and an event occurring without human intervention is a difference in kind and not of degree. Interest in behaviour centres on potentiality, interest in physics on regularities. The appreciation of this difference strengthens the incentive for a change of direction of a technology that is destroying the ground on which it operates. The redirection cannot be achieved unaided. It needs the help of institutions capable of providing a framework and the means for this task. The first step towards this end is to trace the manner in which facts are being described and evidence obtained.

DESCRIPTION OF CHANGE

By treating observables as part of the furniture of the world, they can be itemized. Their description will vary with the particular interest for which it is prepared. According to purpose, features showing differences and similarities between discrete items will be selected and typified by a process of generalization in which the Hereford heifers Betty and Lizzy become "2 cows." In typifying things, an ideation of the actual takes place and description oscillates between these poles of experience.

To describe ideations, metaphors are needed. These link the particularities of a percept to a taxonomy of types. Metaphors used in comprehensive descriptions are not derived directly from the percept of a particular nor can the particular be derived directly from them. In mediating between infinite possibilities of appearance and the possibility of infinity, metaphors acknowledge the debt which ideas owe to facts.

The statement "The sun is appearing on the horizon" includes the surroundings in which an appearance presents itself. Implied in the description of the appearance is the description of a change in appearance. Ongoing change is represented by a description of its phases. A segmentation results which, if left to itself, would obscure the continuity of a change. To strengthen the connection between phases, explanations are inserted. These depend more on interpretation, which cannot stop short of reading between the lines, and they are more open to it than descriptions. Even the most faithful account of change is more than one removed from a simple factual description.

THE SERIATION OF PERCEIVING AND REMEMBERING

A percept does not coincide with its sense datum. A solid box does not show all its sides but its appearance points to those hidden from view as the potentialities of its appearance. They can be ignored only at the risk of destroying the unity of the percept. This unity may be demonstrated in a 360-degree holograph which shows all surfaces simultaneously. This optical simulacrum illustrates the distinction between the appearance of a thing and the experience of the thing appearing.

Things do not appear exclusive of each other. Their plurality is a primary condition of the experience of the world. The ground on which something presents itself forms with it the pattern of "figure on the ground." As part of their surroundings, things share a background or horizon against which they appear. Hence, the basic pattern of a percept is "figure on the ground against a horizon." Any ultimate delimitation against which things appear functions as their horizon. Except in moments of ecstasy, there is always a mundane horizon surrounding the things and the behaviour directed towards them.

In observing something, our glance focuses on it. By this glance, a thing is perceived "in the strong sense," it detaches itself from its background. At the same time, the surroundings consisting of other things nearby and the common background are noticed peripherally, they are perceived "in the weak sense." When attention moves from one thing to another nearby, the latter is now perceived in the strong sense. What has previously been so perceived becomes part of the surroundings. It may remain perceived but only in the weak sense. As the surroundings remain the same, the resulting series of percepts makes sense although casting light on something involves obscuring something else.

The operative terms "figure," "ground" and "horizon" in this account point first to the experience of visual percepts. As none but the simplest things are describable without the help of metaphors, there can be no intrinsic objection to the metaphorical use of these operative terms in describing an auditory experience. There is however the risk that a visual metaphor may not do justice to the overlapping resonances and meaningful intervals characteristic of the auditory "field." This failure in trustworthy description can be acute as undertones exert a more diffused and yet persistent influence on a theme than a background on the figure which is appearing against it. This issue makes itself felt in procedural law where the principle of orality and the maxim *quod non est in actis non est in mundo* oppose each other.

In order to show what is meant by perceiving in the "strong" sense, we have used the expression "to focus one's glance." Yet, while the lens of the eye and the optical lens are similar, the eye is not an instrument but an organ. Even when we gaze "fixedly" at an object, the eye is usually not at rest but performs constantly rapid scanning adjustments. As we are unaware of these probes, our efforts in interpreting a percept are biased towards states of rest, we turn away from the limitless chaos of becoming and seek confirmation of a bound order of being. This bias shapes our fundamental assumptions when we construct models of the world or of any of its parts. These models express our preference for fixed, geometrically determinable boundaries. The same bias is at work when, having projected our visual experience of above and below into the universe where it is without physical meaning, we retrieve these projections in order to validate hierarchical structures of sociality. Again, this visual bias tempts us to consider the world a spectacle to which we relate by means of a proscenium built of hypotheses.

The tendency of granting pre-eminence to expressions based on the experience of visual percepts is the more remarkable as language, the condition which makes our sociality possible, is first of all spoken and heard, not written and read in silence. The "etherealization" of communications, a product of the mathematics of science and technology, has undermined however the pre-eminence of the spoken word and is reinforcing the visual bias. The new advances which electronics have made in voice reproduction and transmission are here offset by the growing number of messages in computer languages which are meant to be silently read, not heard.

The strictures directed at the visual bias culminate in the reproach that literacy provides only a second-rate access to understanding. In the conclusion of Plato's *Phaedrus* the daemon of invention praised writing as his crowning achievement and he counseled the Pharaoh to make all his subjects literate for it would make them more remindful and intelligent. The Pharaoh declined to take this advice on the ground that universal literacy would have the opposite effect.[1] The point is that the use of the alphabet, if not already of hieroglyphs, results in a certain decomposition of the inner unity of the word. In this way an autonomous meaning which a word is capable of carrying may depreciate with the spread of literacy. In "Io" however Plato noted that corybantes dance only to a single tune.[2] Looking at vases which depict these celebrants we can see their self-absorbing fascination as they toss rhythmically their heads without feeling any need of using their eyes. The Greek word for human being, *anthropos*, denotes a being which gives itself an upright stance — to see better what is ahead and above, whereas in order to hear better we may still put an ear close to the ground. And did not Oedipus, on hearing of his past, destroy his sight rather than his hearing?

For the purposes of this inquiry it is not requisite, even if it was possible, to resolve once for all the tension between Apollonian vision and Dionysian sound. It is sufficient here to agree that we should neither surrender ourselves to the visual bias nor push distrust to the logical conclusion of ceasing to use written symbols. We shall encounter a similar dilemma when the problems of diagrammatic representation are being considered.[3]

Only in statements of the type "I see x" is description contemporaneous with perception. Statements of this kind are rarer than those made from recollection. The mere interval between averting one's glance and directing it once more to the same place brings

---

[1] *Phaedrus*, 274c-275b; *cf.*, Letter VII, 343a: "No intelligent man will ever be so bold as to put into language those things which his reason has contemplated, especially not in a form that is unalterable — which must be the case with what is expressed in written symbols."

[2] *Ibid.*, 536c.

[3] See *post*, pp. 46, 48, and 80.

recollection into play. This passage from percept to recollection is a guarantee of the unity of the world as each recollection refers ultimately to the world horizon against which it appears. Percept and its recollection are the minimum conditions which make experience possible. Sharing the same ground and surroundings, or in any case the same horizon, the remembered percept assures that it belongs to the world in which it had been perceived, not merely dreamed or imagined. Something which had been perceived retains its concreteness even in recollection, whereas typically the things which are being imagined or appear in a dream will lack coherent surroundings however vivid the image or dream may have been. They do not show themselves with the world at their horizon.

The things in the world present themselves in serial patterns in which recollections form the antecedents of each actual percept. The selectivity of memory determines the antecedent part of each particular recollections-percept series. This selectivity avoids the chaos which total memory would create. For any aggregate of things there is an indefinite variety of possible recollections-percept series, and their elements cannot be determined in advance. The horizon forms an ultimate surrounding but recedes in the measure one advances towards it, and any lateral delimitation is always provisional. These delimitations bring out patterns of relation between elements of a whole. They show these elements both as distinct appearances and as contributions to the integration of a whole.

The experience of an actual or remembered percept is co-extensive with personal life and thus a lived experience. It is both unique and impersonal. It is unique because it becomes part of a recollections-percept series, the antecedent elements of which are singularly determined by the selectivity of memory. Yet, however singular a lived experience may be, it does not change the appearance of an observable. There is nothing in the description of a simple appearance to show that it presented itself only to a single person, nor does the description point to the possibility of not so appearing to another person, subject always to adjustments or corrections on the non-fulfillment of an expectation.

The corroboration of singular experience is made possible by sociality. It provides the defence against the doubts which the notion of solipsism raises.[4] Moreover, these doubts exhaust themselves in regressive visions that repeat themselves endlessly like a reflection in two opposite mirrors. The statement "it is I who is seeing or imagining this" points to an ego that stands apart from its experience. This has led to the two opposing models of an ego which constitutes its experience and of an ego which is constituted by its experience. Neither construction is based on

---

[4] Cf., Wittgenstein, *Tractatus Logico-Philosophicus* (London, 1922), 5.6-5.641.

evidence, each is speculative and relies for acceptance on a particular world view to which it seeks to conform. Recollection however provides evidence which shows, against the horizon of the historicity of the world, the history of personal experience. This history is, in varying degrees, open to the future and the further course of experience transforms its meaning.

THE HISTORICITY OF BEHAVIOUR

Being directed towards the world, behaviour creates human meanings in it. Past behaviour constitutes itself as history in a world which was always already there. A recollections-percept series manifests history in a present that is being lived. Being present, history does not require a Newtonian type of hypothesis of an "action-at-a-distance." Historicity as human history in general is not dependent on the discovery of a beginning. The more we search for evidence of beginnings, the further they recede into the past. This does not seek to establish that man has an infinite past, only that it is indefinite.

Experiences can be compared but recollections can be shared only rarely as each personal history is different. This is one of the senses in which history cannot be changed however inacceptable it may be. Behaviour, being observable, appears against the common horizon of the human world and in transforming its appearance expresses meanings for the agent and all others. Their content cannot be created by a decision. Behaviour has a presence and thus an expressivity of its own.

A series of behaviours establishes cumulative meanings. Sliding gradually into crime by a series of acts without having a definite criminal plan is an example. A radical break with tradition constitutes itself as such only by reference to the preceding acts in which tradition was followed. Each act, however radically new, gains meanings from the preceding acts and in turn contributes meaning to the acts which follow. Singular history realizes itself in a series of overlapping meanings which explain each other and establish a meaning-context. A proposal to give a definite meaning to one's existence remains however in the realm of imagination. Concrete meanings are created only by transformations of the appearance of the world.

When one looks at a construction site where the foundations of a building are being laid, one may see some workers walking, some driving vehicles, some fastening materials. Their singular behaviour does not disclose the meaning of the common undertaking of "laying the foundations of a building." This meaning is grasped only when the undertaking is viewed as a whole and the singular contributions as its parts. The activity of a group of behaviours has a unity that is anterior to its elements.

What the "sidewalk superintendent" observes is nothing personal. The sidewalk on which he stands, the construction site at which he looks, appear to others as the same sidewalk and the same construction site. For each observer and worker alike, the work appears in the weak sense as the same surroundings, but some elements are from the point of view of each privileged, for instance a concern with unemployment. The characteristics of the work are the same for all, different are the interests of each. When several behaviours are viewed, they appear against the horizon of the singular history of the observer bearing human meanings for him and for the agents as they share the same human world.

"Laying the foundations of a building" is not an isolated event, it is attached to human history in general. It refers to a certain development in techniques and points to certain economic and social factors. This anchors the work in a history which, due to the historicity of each personal life, has a unifying character.

Constellations of co-operation and conflict are summed up in the saying, "I and my tribe against the nation, I and my cousins against my tribe, I and my brothers against my cousins, I against my brothers." The possessive pronouns in the saying show the elements and limiting conditions of social cohesion as each is at the same time a whole and a part of another whole so that self-interest is inadequate to explain singular behaviour. This two-faced character of sociality is reflected in relations of dominance and subservience where the history of the ruled affects the behaviour of the ruler and the history of the ruler the behaviour of the ruled.

It is the task of institutions to direct group behaviour, in situations of co-operation and conflict alike, into familiar channels. Idolatry of institutions provides support in this task but it obstructs the launching of reforms designed to forestall a radicalization of change. The outcome of an encounter between persons or groups is unpredictable but the meaning of a conflict can be found in the resentments over the past behaviour of others which history preserves.

Chapter 2

Systems and Topics

TECHNOLOGICAL BEHAVIOUR

According to Kant, knowledge acquires scientific character only by becoming part of a system, and he defined system as an entirety of knowledge which is ordered according to principles.[1] Technological behaviour is systematized behaviour in construction and destruction. It does not seem to be simply a genetic inheritance, it is planned and its structure is maintained by information which itself is systematic. The realization of a systematic project distinguishes technological from technical behaviour. In technological behaviour, uniformity of results is attributed to successful "rationalization." It begins with the production of uniform tools. Uniformity is sought by describing quality in quantitative terms. Pythagoras heard in the harmony of sound and numbers a "music of the spheres." On the other hand, the shock of the realization that in right triangles the irreducible ratios between the lengths of the sides could be expressed only in "irrational" and not in whole numbers is said to have blocked in antiquity the maximization of technology more effectively than the institution of slavery. The reverberations of a shock running into the opposite direction are now felt by the industrialized world. Having taken the turn which the classical world passed by, the road of technology has led to a giantism that threatens to collapse under its own weight and to bring down the superstructures which it supports.

Technological change redraws the lines between the technologically competent, the obsolescent and the superfluous; it leads to re-divisions of labor and re-distributions of authority. Typically, technological behaviour precedes the effort of scientific measurements as it is ready to take risks which knowledge at hand refuses to accept. The measurements of an established technology however become a source of readily available information on the systematic use of materials and processes.

Techniques of production are made intelligible by the principle of causality. Aspects of this principle are the properties of the material as *causa materialis*, the shape the article takes as *causa formalis* and its purpose as *causa finalis*. Systematization defines and confines the variables for each cause and their interrelations. In technology, the

---

[1] *Metaphysical Foundations of Natural Science,* Preface p. iv.

behaviour of the maker as *causa efficiens* is reduced to the level of the other three causes. This demotion is the result of the separation of planning from production. The separation is part of inherent tendencies towards maximization. At present, it is achieved by substituting automated machines for the personal skills which the use of handtools require.[2] The planner of means of production becomes the model of technological man, the actual maker an assembler of parts or a minder of machines. Production is experienced indirectly and the historicity of production becomes irrelevant, leaving no one and everyone to blame for the bad faith with which goods are produced and consumed. The aim of technology to do more with less has resulted in doing less with more.

FAMILIARITY

Recurrencies of fulfilled expectations breed familiarity. Characteristic of daily life is a familiarity with one's surroundings. A task which has become familiar can however be performed also in different surroundings. The task serves as reference point from which the relevance of changes in the surroundings can be gauged.

Once a routine for the performance of a task is established, decisions are no longer needed to determine the various steps involved or the sequence in which they are to be taken. Unless routines turn into rituals, they have an inbuilt resilience that enables them to absorb changes which occur between one set of routine acts and its repetition. If a new appearance fulfills an expectation that leaves the meaning context of the surroundings intact, the change is not a change of the familiar but a familiar change.

Systems are elaborations of routines. Habitual behaviour reinforces itself whilst the integrity of a system depends on its logical cohesion. The directing theme of a system aligns the consistency of the system elements with its purpose. Similar to an efficient cause, the directing theme acts on the system from the outside. It straddles the boundaries in which the system is designed to operate.

A system prescribes the behaviour which operates it. Unless controlled, behaviour tends to push through the limits of the regulating prescriptions of the system. The contest between behaviour and its regulation calls for the interpretation of both. The interpretation depends on the evidential and semantic relevances of the situation in which the contest takes place.

---

[2] According to an article in *B.C. Lumberman,* August 1974, p. 22, entitled "The 'idiot-proof' Skidder," "... the basic concept is to make (skidders) so fool-proof that even the greenest operator can run the machine." Skidders are tractors which drag logs from the stump to the haulage road.

SWEEPING CHANGE

Feed-back arrangements provide systems with stabilizing immunities against change. When change amounts to a perturbation of the system, it needs relaxation time to return to normal. If the increase in the rate of change exceeds a certain limit, which typically cannot be determined in advance, the relaxation time needed becomes longer than the interval between perturbations.[3] In this radical change, the system becomes unstable. Dynamic reverberations of increasing frequencies may make the instability permanent, leading to a collapse. In situations of stress, systems reveal their Achilles heel: the inability to be both consistent and complete.

A disappearance of familiar landmarks is a symptom of sweeping change. It brings doubts whether means of dealing with a new situation are at hand. A problem presents itself. It may not be solvable if interpretation proceeds within a network of meanings designed on systematic-deductive lines. In this method of reasoning, questions and answers are selected from within the system. Being dependent on it, interpretation is led in a direction which has been legislated in advance. Compliance with a system in the face of sweeping change demands a belief similar to that of the Etruscans of whom Seneca wrote: "They believe not that [events] have significance because they have occurred but that they have occurred because they have significance."[4] Here, uncertainty is converted into certainty in straightlined operations which are well described by the phrase "to figure out something." It is the antithesis of the deviousness with which historicity traces its path.[5]

If problems due to a sweeping change are met head-on, they may turn out to be insoluble. An indirect approach is more rewarding. It begins with the search for relevances. The directing theme of the system is bracketed out and all efforts are concentrated on finding means of overcoming or circumventing the obstacle which the problem represents. Before entering on this path, one cannot predict the prospects of success or the new problems that the solution of the present one may bring to light. Yet, in contrast to the decision made on systematic-deductive lines, problem solving can claim a mere alleviation of symptoms or the gain of a respite as a success.

---

[3] Stafford Beer, *Designing Freedom* (Toronto: C.B.C. Publications, 1978), chapters I and II.
[4] *Naturales Quaestiones* II, 32,2.
[5] On justiciary perturbations see R. W. M. Dias, "The Law at the End of its Tether," [1972] *Cambridge Law Journal* 293-319.

PROBLEM SOLVING

To make the unfamiliar intelligible, several viewpoints are taken to link an unfamiliar appearance to familiar elements in the surroundings. These include the notions which are associated with them. This topical[6] approach seeks views that reach beyond the operational concepts to which a system is bound by its design. Topics point to clues for a solution of a problem. As viewpoints, they may be listed but their catalogue cannot be ordered into lines of subordination. Problem solving involves moving from one topic to another and to pursue the ramifications of a problem that at first sight appeared as a single obstacle. Reasoning according to topics does not provide a method in the sense of a systematic procedure, but lacking it, the reasoning will be free of the risks peculiar to systematizations. One of the gravest of these risks arises from the tendency towards maximization. Giantism, the defiance of the human scale, renders lines of communication tenuous and distorts the messages which circulate through the system.

The array of notions in a topic is held together by the evocative strength of their association. One of these may have a particular affinity to one aspect of the problem. The affinity makes this aspect relevant to the topic and the topic relevant to the aspect. Relevance is discovered not by proceeding from the known to the unknown or from the unknown to the known but by an analogy in which neither the thing to be compared nor its counterpart is determined until they are actually matched. Finding the relevant is the first step in linking the problematic to the familiar. The matching of a topical element with an element of a problem is made possible by lived experience. Topics as tools of solving problems of human behaviour will be successful to the degrees to which a lived experience can come near claiming: *Homo sum, humani nil a me alienum puto.*

The questions and answers of a topical approach depend on an assessment of degrees of probability and plausibility. Ultimately, the answer is governed by the persuasiveness of the description or judgment. To be plausible calls for an explicit or silent assent to the description of the surroundings of a problem. Their boundaries are likely to be blurred and the assent is often general rather than specific.

---

[6] On topics see Julius Stone, *Legal System and Lawyers' Reasoning* (London, 1964), pp. 331-2; Ch. Perelman, *The Idea of Justice and the Problem of Argument*, intr. H.L.A. Hart (London, 1963), pp. vii-xi, 138, 152, 158; T. Viehweg, *Topik und Jurisprudenz* (Muenchen, 1965), 3rd ed., pp. 1, 16-26; S.E. Toulmin, *The Uses of Argument* (Cambridge, 1958), referring on pp. 7-8, 15-17, 41-3, 96, 141-2 to legal reasoning calls for a "rapprochement" between logic and epistemology with history presiding over their amalgamation (p. 254); Otto Bird, "The Re-Discovery of Topics: Prof. Toulmin's Inference-Warrants" (1961), 70 *Mind* 534-9, places Toulmin in the role of a Monsieur Jourdain for having failed to realize that he was talking topics until the author told him so.

Assent gives topics a social dimension and, involving behaviour, it invokes its historicity.

The problem may not lie in one single element of a situation but in the configurations of its elements. In this case, the problem solving task begins with the recognition of patterns of relations. In this topical approach, several relevances present themselves. The reason for rejecting some is not that they do not make sense but that alternative relevances make better sense. There is the objection to the topical approach that a description has to analyse before it can totalize. The objection rests on belief. Even Pascal's "wager" that one would be wise to believe, since in the end the believer will lose nothing and the unbelievers everything, would not settle the matter as long as one can believe either that language is logic or logic linguistics. This uncertainty may make the description of a problem solving task more complex than the task itself. On the other hand, description on systematic-deductive lines increases the disorientation which occurs on encountering a sweeping change.

A system depends on distinct boundaries between its elements. The boundaries are best safeguarded by definitions which follow the rules of extensional logic. These will permit unambiguous answers if the definitions form the building blocks of a closed system or if accepted standards of measurements produce quantifications. In contrast, topics are quality oriented so that evaluation has to supplement or take the place of analysis. Qualities transcend the boundaries which define and confine system elements as value is diffused, and the value of a whole is not necessarily the same as the sum of the values of its parts. Although different styles of reasoning are involved, it would be rash to consider system builders hardheaded and problem solvers softhearted. Also, either may well be both softheaded and hardhearted.

Standards make general judgments possible. Sociality sets standards of behaviour. The justice meted out if a particular behaviour fails to meet expectations protects social balances. On encountering sweeping change, ideologies seek to displace morals. They are simplified programmes for the realization of abstractions and their simplicity makes them useful as promises. Like scientific hypotheses, they are replaceable.[7] To qualify a conviction as ideological, it should be strong enough to thrust aside the doubts in which alternative interpretations of a situation present themselves. Fanaticism does not bear the entire blame for the ideological reaction to doubt. In a wider sense it reflects the problem of the equivalence of the actual with its abstraction. Each ideology implies its antithesis. Their contests lead to re-distributions of

---

[7] An example from science is the replacement of species-oriented Darwinism by neo-Darwinism. For a critique of the quantitative approach of this theory see Marjorie Grene, *The Knower and the Known* (London, 1966), pp. 253-266.

authority and re-divisions of labour. Motives of behaviour are mixed, and ideology seeks to abolish their ambivalence. Yet, typically, in situations of radical change, what each singular person aims for is obstructed by everyone else and what emerges is something no one expected.

The ultimate aim of a system is to provide security amidst change, and the attraction of a system may even be strengthened instead of weakened by its inability to cope with change. System building is not deterred by the conflicts which arise between competing systems as each promises an order and its certainties. In contrast, problem-solving is haunted by the foreknowledge that the solution of a present problem is likely to produce another one. To build a system may require more energy than finding topics, but in its application a system can save energy while problem solving consumes it. However, when change acquires an unexpected momentum, a problem that has been solved provides a cushion between the dismantling of one system and the construction of another one. Even this short-term aim requires an institutional framework for the control of the problem-solving task. If during the intermediate period the old system is preserved for the performance of familiar tasks, the insertion of the solution of the problem into the system will have to be well timed so that the solution will not inhibit the operation of the system or the system the realization of the solution. Last but not least, problem solving calls for an attitude of watchful patience, an attitude which fosters respect for the law, not its disregard.

ORDER

Systematization brings order. In an anthropological view, "order represents a state of purity which is the enemy of change, of ambiguity and compromise."[8] A pure and simple appearance owes everything to itself and nothing to its surroundings. The more pure and simple the system elements, the more orderly will be the appearance of the system. Purity and simplicity may however manifest themselves on the surface only, and scrutiny will uncover the hidden impurities and complexities. Inversely, disorder is associated with dirt, and dirt with misbehaviour. Beyond a certain degree of disorder, institutions can no longer respond to the behaviours they are designed to direct.[9] The more the pollution of behaviours and surroundings manifests the disorganization of a systematic order, the more intense becomes the urge to regain a purity which in recollection tends to appear free of all rigidities, contradictions

---

[8] Mary Douglas, *Purity and Danger* (London, 1966), pp. 5, 91-5, 191.
[9] *Ibid.*, pp. 119, 123 and 162.

and hypocrisy. Even if these flaws are remembered, they appear as a lesser threat to security than the possibility of total pollution.

The desire for purity of order shows itself in attitudes towards the paradoxes of logic. There is a tendency to look upon paradoxes as disorders which can be swept away like leavings. Characteristic is a comment on paradoxical "counterfactuals": "But such cases do not argue insolubility; for if we can provide an interpretation that handles the clear cases successfully, we can let the unclear ones fall where they may."[10] However, unclear cases may have no alternative but to fall back into the logical system in which they arose. Further on the paradox of negation and the inherent inconsistency of systems will be considered.[11] There, affinities between the unclear, the impure and the disorderly will become further apparent. On the present topic of order, the notion of entropy as the movement of system elements towards disorder becomes significant. In entropy the opposites of order and disorder as well as those of clarity and opacity, purity and impurity are drawn together. Goodman's unclear, paradox cases point to an entropy within logic itself.

The re-establishment of systematic order should not be confounded with the restoration of the old. The assessment of the chances which favour restoration is ultimately based on a Laplacean type of probability theory in which no event is being treated as unique and every event as repetition of a former one. Strictly speaking however no repetition is the same as its predecessor if only because it is a repetition, nor are there inherent limitations on the possibility of building systems which differ from each other. Moreover, lived experience transforms by re-interpretation even the most faithful attempt at restoration.

It does not follow that, except for the period of an interregnum, problem solving has to yield to system building. Systems seek to control human behaviour but the control cannot be a total one. Problem solving will always have a place in the order of things even when order is not threatened by radical change. System builders and problem solvers are competitors. Their co-existence cannot be fully harmonized as they are affected by mutual interpenetrations which imbalance both the system and the problem-solving task.

---

[10] Nelson Goodman, *Fact, Fiction and Forecast*, 3rd ed. (Indianapolis, 1973), p. XIII.
[11] See *post* pp. **40** and **57** .

Chapter 3

Scrutinizing

WHOLES AND PARTS

The discreteness of a whole shows itself in its spatial and temporal distances from another whole. Distances are measurable so that the appearance of a whole has a quantifiable character which absorbs the character of the parts. At the same time, a whole can show itself as a configuration of elements. If a part is taken away from the whole, the whole is diminished but the part retains its character as a part. If an element is taken away from a configuration, the element loses its character as element but the configuration persists if the relevant elements are retained. In this way, institutions retain their status even if membership changes. The integrity of an institution shows a continuity which is comparable to the coherence of a recollections-percept series which persists even if elements of the series change.

The riddle of the "sorites" or heap, which the Ancients posed, shows the quantitative aspect of the problem of continuity. The riddle runs: "This is a heap of grain; take away one grain — two grains — three grains, and so on — is it still a heap?" The problem lies not in the number of grains but in their configuration as a whole. The riddle relies on the possibility of reducing a whole in a series of minute steps. Each grain has inherently the potency of destroying the configuration but the actual grain which will achieve this is not identifiable in advance. In illustrating the notion of continuity, the riddle points also to the distinction between extensional and intensional judgments.

QUANTIFICATION AND MEANING

Quantification is the dominant characteristic of technology. A steady chorus of protests accompanies its achievements. Dickens' *Hard Times* describes it all.[1] In linguistic behaviour, quantification seeks to emancipate meaning from its context of surroundings and history. This emancipation requires a metasystem of norms of interpretation. The metasystem can, however, rest only on another one so that infinite

---

[1] For an overview of this criticism of the doctrine of materialism see Edgar Johnson, *Charles Dickens* (New York, 1952), Vol. II pp. 801-819; Darwin's *Descent of Man*, 1871, forms the main plank of this doctrine.

regress is created. Even so, the serial character of linguistic behaviour points to a semantic calculus which produces results that are not wholly trivial.

Most speech consists of sentences that have not been used before. Their information may be measured in terms of the uncertainty which the message events remove. The degree of uncertainty may be considered a function of the probability of the occurrence of a particular symbol in comparison with others which might have been chosen. If an unlikely symbol is received, it conveys more information than one which was highly probable. This is to say, if nothing new is stated, no uncertainty is removed. The probability assessment is assisted by the circumstance that common speech, whether it is descriptive or normative, determines what commonly can be said and how to say it in or about a given situation. In this sense, common speech is a restricted code. Its repertoire is limited and redundancy by repetition is characteristic of it. Redundancy provides a quantifiable basis for the interpretational relevances of the elements of a message. The decrease of the average uncertainty of the symbols used is a measure of the increase in redundancy. The greater the redundancy of symbols, the less information the message provides, and the less the information, the greater the intensity of the meaning of the message. Meaning is here understood as that which makes sense of the message.[2] Redundancy is therefore a means of increasing the coherence between successive statements. It provides familiar surroundings for the prime constituent part of the message.

However, while the relations between redundancy, information and meaning have quantitative aspects, this is not the case for the relation between meaning and interpretational imagination as the latter is dependent on the histories of the agent and of the interpreter, a relation which is not quantifiable. Interpretation is governed by the relative adequacy of the probability of competing alternatives, and the problems of quantification which appear in theories of probability reappear in theories of interpretation.

PROBABILITY AND TRUTH

Possibility impels desire, probability behaviour. Behaviour seeks to realize whatever seems possible and to justify itself according to degrees of probability. Possibility includes that which is barely possible. A bare or simple possibility is only one remove from the notion of accident.[3]

---

[2] See F.C. Crosson, "Information Theory," in *Philosophy and Cybernetics*, Crosson and Sayre, eds. (New York, 1968), pp. 102, 108, 114, 118 and 127.

[3] A.P. Herbert, *Uncommon Law* (London, 1935), p. 316 defined an act of God as "something which no reasonable man could have expected."

Moreover, what is barely possible includes the possibility of being impossible. When something that was considered barely possible happens, it will appear to have been no more and no less than a proper possibility, and if an attempt to realize a simple possibility fails, to have been impossible. This is the weakness at the lower end of the scale of hypothetical behaviour and the source of all doubts on the prospects of a success.

The notion of probability is more rewarding. Current views distinguish three aspects of probability: Relative frequency, degree of confirmation and personal probability.[4] Each of the theories which centre on these aspects of probability has fundamental limitations that cannot be eliminated by combining some of their diverse elements. The most common fallacy in assessing a probability in terms of relative frequency is to use a given frequency ratio magnitude as being determinative of the degree of probability. The generalization following an expressed relative frequency ratio, this is to say a quantification, beyond the observed cases requires the support from the evidence of the observed cases. This support however cannot itself be explained in terms of relative frequencies and indeed cannot be expressed in numerical terms at all; it can be characterized only by such expressions as "strong," "adequate," "weak" and so on.[5]

Further, what amounts to sufficient confirmation for multi-predicate elements will ultimately depend on

> reasonable and knowledgeable persons when confronted with the question of ascertaining a value [of the degree of confirmation computed according to a hypothesis and evidence finding] this computation definitely, if vaguely, meaningful and [arriving] at estimates of the value that will not be too widely disparate.[6]

As typically the elements of a human situation are multi-predicative, and the relevance of the evidence is determined by the hypothesis involved, the utility of the "degree of confirmation" approach weakens with the degree of esoterism of the knowledge required.

Last, the "personal probability" theory reduces itself to betting behaviour. It depends on the "rationality" of the agent, in particular on his receptivity to new relevant evidence and his indifference "as to which side to take in a bet that to his knowledge is a 'fair' bet."

The shortcomings of current theories are serious enough to justify a return to earlier efforts. Carneades (214-129 B.C.) was one of the first who saw in probability the criterion for the meaning of actual and prospective behaviour. In his long career as head of the New Academy

---

[4] See Nicholas Rescher, *Scientific Explanations* (New York, 1970), Appx. II, para. 6, pp. 179 ss.
[5] See P.F. Strawson, *Introduction to Logical Theory* (London, 1963), pp. 237 ss.
[6] Rescher, *supra*, n. 4, p. 182.

and its most famous teacher, he preferred lecturing to writing. The recording of his life work was left to his disciple and successor, the Carthaginian Hasdrubal, who taught and wrote and under his Greek name Clitomachus. This record, consisting of 40 rolls, has been lost. Yet, Carneades' fame lasted throughout antiquity and many references to his teachings are found in classical literature. One of the best known of these was provided by Cicero who praised him as "a man of the greatest genius and acuteness."[7] Cicero's philosophical writings suffered, however, from the pressures of his political misfortunes even if they allowed him time for study and writing. Sextus Empiricus (ca. 200 A.D.),[8] provides a more extensive and more discerning account of Carneades' work. Some passages in this account appear to be paraphrases or even quotations taken verbatim from the rolls of Clitomachus.

Following the nomenclature of the ancients, Carneades and Sextus Empiricus are widely considered as leading exponents of skepticism. It would be more accurate however to see Carneades as a Phenomenalist. It is conceded that the ubiquity of doubt was the central theme of his relentless attacks on Stoic doctrines. However brilliant these attacks were, in the end they proved to have been made in vain as the teachings of the Stoa prevailed and the New Academy turned to Neo-Platonism. Carneades should be considered a Phenomenalist rather than a Skeptic because the doubts he raised were not directed to the content of the sense datum but to its meaning. In this sense, the usual riposte to skepticism "If everything is to be doubted, this proposition also is to be doubted" fails against Carneades. His achievements are worth considering. He moved *aporetics*, the unravelling of problems, from the margin to the centre of philisophizing and was the first to stress the importance of behaviour in problem solving.

The origins and background of Carneades and Sextus Empiricus are significant. Both came from distant overseas colonies to spend their creative years in metropolitan centres. Translocation heightens the attentiveness to change in which the familiar becomes strange and the strange familiar. The historical moments in which these two men lived are also relevant. During Carneades' lifetime, the Greek city states became entirely dependent on Roman power. With this dependence, the glory that was classical Greece finally departed. Sextus Empiricus, separated by four centuries from Carneades, lived under the reign of the successors of Marcus Aurelius, emperor, Stoic philosopher and persecutor of Christians. During the reign of unworthy successors, the empire underwent a century-long spasm of civil wars and disorders.

---

[7] *De Re Publica III*, 7; see also Plutarch, *Twelve Lives* (Cleveland, 1950), pp. 383-4.
[8] *Sextus Empiricus*, tr. and ed. by R.G. Bury (London, 1961); for an evaluation of the epistemological aspects of this work see C.L. Hamblin, *Fallacies* (London, 1970), pp. 246-7, 250, 295-8.

Parallels with these times of trouble give to the views of Carneades a special poignancy. History relives itself to the extent that its lessons are not learned.

Carneades' example of the snake is a key to his views on probability and relevance:

> On seeing a coil of rope in an unlighted room a man jumps over it, conceiving it for the moment to be a snake, but turning back afterwards he enquires into the truth, and on finding it motionless he is already inclined to think that it is not a snake, but as he reckons all the same, that snakes too are motionless at times when numbed by winter's frost, he prods at the coiled mass with a stick, and then, after thus testing the presentation received, he assents to the fact that it is false to suppose that the body presented to him is a snake.[9]

This episode, trivial as at first it may appear, gains in meaning by the contrast between the security offered by a house, a step in the development of civilizing techniques, and the limitations of all technical measures of security. At a further level, the example shows the contrast between a reactive behaviour of aggression attributed to the reptile and the reflective attitude of the householder who refrains from forestalling an attack by an equally blind pre-emptive strike.

The passage appears to be a direct quotation from Clitomachus. The expression "the truth" in the translation of this passage calls for some comment. Originally, this term denoted "plighted faith." This meaning survived in the verb "to betroth"[10] but in the noun only to the extent that truth is something to which one will swear.[11] In the current meaning of truth as the opposite of falsity or as synonym of the real the connotation of a personal commitment has been largely eroded.[12] In the Greek text, the expression translated as "the truth" is *talēthes*.[13] The intrinsic meaning of this absolute adjective is that which is or rather is becoming unconcealed.[14]

There is an affinity between *talēthes* and the original meaning of relevance. The Greek expression denotes the uncovering of a thing which is veiled or otherwise hidden from view. "Relevance" in its

---

[9] *Ibid.*, "Against the Logicians," I, 187-9 (Vol. II pp. 100-103); see also *ibid.* "Outlines of Pyrrhonism," I, 227-8 (Vol. I pp. 138-141), "Against the Professors," II, 63-4 (Vol. IV pp. 219-221) and "Against the Logicians," I, 185-6 (II pp. 99-100).

[10] See *S.O.E.D.*, 3rd ed., 2375 and 186.

[11] It is in this sense of a sworn commitment to the fact-finding task that the verdict (*vere dictum*) should be understood. The diffused character of the commitment explains the difficulty of instructing the jury on the difference between reasonable and unreasonable doubt.

[12] For a survey of current views on the truth problem see Michael Dummett, "Truth" in a collection of essays bearing the same title, George Pitcher, ed. (Englewood, New Jersey, 1964), pp. 95-111.

[13] The first letter in *talēthes* is the elided definite article.

[14] Liddell and Scott, 9th ed., p. 64.

original meaning denotes the lifting up of a thing, to bring it to prominence, so that it can be seen better.

As it is frequently the case, the translation of *talēthes* as "the truth" fails to exhibit all the semantic implications of the original. What is obscured is the problem solving character of a behaviour designed to gain information on a range of probabilities.[15]

As the reader of this passage may not be well acquainted with the ways of snakes, he should note that it is safer to jump over a snake which motionlessly blocks the way than it is to retreat. Had the dimly perceived mass been lying in a corner of the room, the man could not have jumped over it. If it was a coiled rope, it was out of place; one does not often leave a coiled rope by itself in the middle of a room. Expecting a familiar scene, the man encounters the unfamiliar, the problematic.

However provisional the identification of the mass as a poisonous snake had to be for want of sufficient illumination, it was the safer of the probable alternatives. The possibility of a snake bite is however not sufficient to justify the jump. Probabilities have to be assessed, otherwise no risk would ever be acceptable. Typically, entering a room is a routine matter. The appearance of the mass in conjunction with its location turned a routine into a problem-solving task.

In problem solving, experience formed in recollections-percept series is the point of departure and the aim is the choice of the behaviour which is appropriate to a concrete situation. The assessment of its probabilities evolves in stages from the scrutiny of the situation to the inquiry into alternative probabilities which present themselves, the determination of their relative degrees, the rejection of some alternatives *ab initio* and of others after further determination, to the testing of the alternatives which remain and the evaluation of the test. This account does not purport to be a prescription of the sequential order in which these steps are to be taken. They may be retraced, their sequence changed or several of them concentrated in a leap in which simultaneity replaces a sequence.

RELEVANCE

Rejection of alternative probabilities is made on a scrutiny of the elements of a situation. The Greek term for scrutiny was *periodomenē* which literally means "walking around" in order to inspect all its aspects. Today, circumspect behaviour means to act with circumspection. The original meaning of this expression is "to look around." What one looks for in looking around are relevances, for instance whether there are hidden aspects of an appearance which

---

[15] For a further example of this discrepancy see n. 8, "Against the Logicians," I 437 (Vol. II pp. 234-5).

could match those expectations that are based on experience. In scrutinizing, one looks for confirmatory evidence of the percept of a thing. This evidence is obtained by rejecting alternatives of probability and interpreting the percept in the light of the remaining alternative.

The subsequent test with the stick in the example of the snake illustrates the rejection, upon scrutiny, of an alternative probability. Wherever the stick was applied to the mass, the probability is that the mass will move under the impact of the stick. Experience shows a difference between the motion made by an inert coil of rope and that of a snake, however torpid the animal may be. Yet, the illumination in the room could have been too dim to discern this difference regardless of the place to which the stick was applied. Suppose however experience shows that a torpid snake needs a certain time to reach a state of alertness. Suppose further that the mass forms a heap. If it was a snake, there is a probability that its head was at the top of the heap. If the stick is being inserted between the top and the rest of the mass, the top end could be raised by lifting the stick. If the mass was a rope, the probability is that the top end will slide off the stick and fall back onto the rest of the mass. If the mass was a snake, the probability is that lifting its head with the stick will arouse the animal, and even if the head will slide off the stick, it will not simply fall back onto the mass but assume a more upright position than before. Hence, the location of the terminals of the mass is relevant to the assessment of probability of the problematic situation in which the man found himself.

Scrutiny is the basis for the assessment of probabilities, and the probable is a criterion of the relevant. Their relation needs further consideration.

Although the Stoics were committed to a view of the world in which truth reveals itself through reason, they allowed for a gap between a truth and its enunciation.[16] This gap became for the Stoics the space for the probable. In this view, the probable is no more than the mediator between the percept and the truth. This was the reason for which the Stoics concentrated their interest on the subsumption of facts to laws conceived as the partial manifestation of a universal law that is demonstrable in propositional logic. Stoics moved therefore with confidence from physics to physiology and from physiology to psychology.

This tradition ceased when the natural philosopher became a scientist. Today, leaving aside attempts at a new synthesis, for instance in socio-biology, each discipline determines the thematization of its objects of knowledge and sets its own frame of reference. Yet, none is

---

[16] Leon Robin, *Pyrrhon et le Scepticisme Grec* (Paris, 1944), p.102; this work contains an exposition of the views of Carneades which is superior to much else that has been written on him.

capable of proving its foundations; there is not sufficient evidence for the thesis that each is an articulation of a unitary, all-embracing science. The operational terms of several disciplines may be homogeneous but their meaning different, and a hypothesis established in one field meaningless in another. The field of a scientific discipline, being marked out by means of its thematic orientation, is made familiar by the method which each discipline determines on its own. Familiarization is achieved by treating methodical steps as elements of a system of operational concepts. As long as the system deals with familiar appearances, it will show the relevance of the operational concept in the repetitions of its application. Change sees to it however that strange appearances will present themselves in the familiar field. If the system failed to provide for them, for instance by feedback arrangements, or otherwise malfunctions, for instance by mistaking the strange for the familiar, the situation becomes problematic. The solution of the problem demands a fresh assessment of relevances. The position in routine behaviour is similar.

A problematic situation is a whole but it is not monolithic; its history ensures that it consists of elements. It is among the elements of a whole that the choice of relevances is made. The double aspect of an appearance had been considered in the first part of this chapter. The appearance can be viewed either as a part of a whole or as an element of it.[17] A distinction can be made between elements whose removal from the whole would lead to the dissolution of the configuration which the whole presents and those elements whose removal would not affect the whole as configuration. To refer again to the example of Carneades, as it has been interpolated here, a snake which loses its head loses its configuration as snake. Hence, if the test with the stick had been directed to the head of the snake, it was a relevant test which led to a conclusive choice between alternative probabilities and thus to the solution of the problem. Accordingly, a relevant element has a latent virtuality to dissolve by separation the configuration of the whole to which it belongs. It is here that topics come into their own as relevance may shift with the change of topics.

This hypothetical detachment of a relevant element bears similarity to the use of a *condicio sine qua non* or necessary condition as test of a causal connection.[18] However, the relation between a relevant element and the problematic situation to which it belongs is not of a causal character and it can be considered functional only in the weak sense.

It can be seen that although the improbable is irrelevant, the probable by itself is not the measure of the relevant. Further, in the example of

---

[17] See *supra*, p. 17.
[18] For some of the problematics of the notion of necessity see Arthur Prior, *Past, Present and Future* (Oxford, 1967), pp. 113-20.

Carneades as here interpolated, certain subordinated themes are being brought forward by the main theme, the assessment of the probability of danger. This transformation of probable relevance into relevant probability is characteristic of problem solving tasks. If the problem arises from human behaviour, the solution shows the particular meaning of the behaviour.

DESCRIBING

The aim of the foregoing descriptions was to determine the primary conditions which make a finding of fact possible. A survey of case and statute law would not be able to show whether a rule of procedure or evidence is meeting the present needs of adjudication. The reported facts of a case and the fact content of a rule are norm-oriented. Hence relevance is prejudged, and a survey of this kind would lack the criteria it needs. These can be found only in the general conditions which make a finding of fact possible. To determine these is, itself, a fact-finding task.

On reviewing the several descriptions in the preceding sections, the question arises whether the connection between them could have been made immediately explicit by invoking a principle capable of prescribing the sequence in which the descriptions were to appear or whether, as will be outlined here, the requisite of trustworthiness speaks against this possibility.

The consideration of this alternative leads back to the subject with which these inquiries began, the theories of the deep structure of the world. It is not a coincidence that the preceding descriptions reflect one of the most important theses of physics, the indeterminacy principle of Heisenberg. He showed that there is no way of devising a method of pinpointing the position of a sub-atomic "particle" unless one is willing to be quite uncertain as to its exact motion and vice versa. The most important consequences of the indeterminacy principle were the abandonment of causality as principle and its replacement by one of the various modern theories of probability. There have been attempts to save the principle of causality by the argument that it is only the presence of the observer which interferes in the process of measurement. It has been found impossible however to overcome this interference and it cannot be determined mathematically.

These results impose fundamental restraints on describing a state of affairs. The long efforts of science at delimitation culminated in discovering our limitations. The same syndrome is being encountered in the paradoxes of logic and the frustrations of system building. More will be said on this later. If these limitations are inherent, they would contradict the view that the experienced finitude of man is counterbalanced by his infinite possibilities. However this may be, the particular significance of these limits lies not in the question whether they are provisional but that they obtrude in all but the most commonplace instances of scientific evidence.

It seems that, except for the changeover to farming in neolithic times and the foundation of the first empires which continuous-yield agriculture made possible, the ongoing increase in the present rate of change is unprecedented. But even should this claim be one of conceit or a sign of panic instead of serious concern, the increase is substantial enough to recommend a fresh look at the grounds on which a finding of fact relies. If one wishes to give our age a single characterizing predicate, no better choice can be made than that of "scientific age" unless one prefers "technological age" in view of the speed-up in development. Concerns about fact finding in general come to a sharp, nagging point when we consider the rules which govern the taking of scientific evidence in adjudication.

The indeterminacy principle had a greater, though less obvious impact than Einstein's theory of special relativity. While this theory called for revisions of the Newtonian model, it still kept close as it protected the view that measurement was everywhere the guarantor of the reliability of a finding of fact, that quantification "hardens" a fact. However, the indeterminacy principle or principle of imprecision, as it has sometimes been called, strengthened the conviction that even in natural science there are things worth knowing which are not describable in quantitative terms.

In looking at the history of modern physics we find that only half a century ago the experiments of Rutherford gave scientists grounds for representing the microcosm in a diagrammatic form that, in its precision, resembled the Newtonian model of the macrocosm. The advent of the indeterminacy principle formed here an historical watershed. The view of the world suggested by the experiments of Rutherford remained in line with a long tradition which began with the atomic doctrine of Democritus and its elaboration in the didactic work of Lucretius, *De Rerum Naturae*. We are not concerned here with its hypotheses of the indestructibility and indivisibility of the atom but with the governing theme of the doctrine: The fundamental orderliness and regularity of Nature — a characteristically Roman notion. Looking at Rome's civilizatory achievement which gave clear expression to the theme, one can say that it mediated between opposing cosmologies, that of Parmenides, the first great conceptualist, who held that it is love which "makes the world go round," and that of Heraclitus who named war or strife the father of all things.

An observer of the decisive change which scientific theory underwent with the advent of the indeterminacy principle might have predicted that it would generate wide distrust of measurement and quantification. In one of the ironic turns, which human history allows itself, the opposite occurred in practice, and in the intervening decades science and technology produced more quantifications than ever. They now affect a wide range of decision-making and other behaviour, and the consequences are being observed over the entire globe and beyond it.

In this situation, the institutions in our superstructures which are charged with fact-finding tasks are facing a new dilemma. While confidence in discovering general truths by the method of quantification was shaken, adjudications of the widest public interest concern fact complexes which require for their interpretation the help of scientific expertise. The technological performance as part of an issue of fact is being assessed by reference to a scientific theory, seemingly dominated by its quantitive aspects, whereas the adjudicator in his efforts to bridge the gap between rule and concrete case cannot dispense with quality-oriented assessments.

We have seen that problem solving with the help of topics comes to the fore whenever the strange is being encountered and that in this mode of fact finding several viewpoints are taken in order to arrive at determinations. The process which is here at work is one of cumulation. It is the same process by which circumstantial evidence is established. There, the sum of the probative values of the parts of the evidence is not necessarily the same as the probative value of the whole evidence. This is to say that this value is not determinable by quantification. In establishing circumstantial evidence the decision on the value of a single item of evidence is suspended until all other items which seem relevant have been scrutinized. In this scrutiny one will go back to an item that had been examined already in order to compare and match it with the other items so as to discover the meanings which they have in common. The issue of fact to be decided by circumstantial evidence is treated as a problem that demands solution and the topical mode of problem solving provides the means for this task.

In contrast, in a description which invokes or implies the principle of causality there is an orderly progression of cause-effect/cause-effect concatenations. The "cause/effect" integration gives the entire narrative a seamless coherence and yet permits measurement of the strength of the postulated causal bond in each cause-effect element. With the downfall of the principle of causality these advantages have been lost. Nor can probability assessments made in quantitative terms take the place of causality as fundamental defects mar the various quantitative theories of probability on which the assessments rely for their authority.

This has a bearing on the form of a description. In the causal mode the narrative moved in a straight line. The several cause-effect elements are contiguous as the effect of a cause is the cause of a subsequent effect. "For want of a shoe the horse was lost; and for want of a horse the rider was lost." In this type of narrative there is never the need to hark back to a cause-effect element that had already been described.

It is different when the topical mode of description is being used. There, as already mentioned, an item or scintilla of evidence will be considered first in the perspective which one topic will offer and then be put aside to make room for other items that will be considered under the same topic. Further, this process will be repeated as often as other topics are being introduced until all appropriate topics seem exhausted. The line followed in this type of inquiry is not a straight line but it turns, helically, back on itself to retrieve a previously considered item or a topic for re-appraisal whereupon it resumes the original direction of the inquiry. If the description suppresses this aspect of the fact finding task in favour of the simplifications of the straight line, characteristic of the causal mode of description, criteria of trustworthiness become concealed, and the author of the account cannot be made accountable for his findings.

On the other hand, if the links between elements of a whole and between wholes are being recognized or discovered with the help of topics, they will point to the relevance of affinities or incompatibilities which permit the drawing of analogies or the determination of a novel and therefore strange configuration. To be trustworthy, this type of fact-finding will include a description of these processes of recognition or discovery, and the description will not be restrained in its sequentiality by pre-ordained priorities as is the case for a description made in causal terms.

A description of the latter kind asserts the rationality of its determinations by a cluster of key terms which show each element to fit precisely into place in an interlocking, conceptual scheme. The mode of description becomes systematized. Certain criticisms of a system building have already been made and they will be strengthened later on by a thesis of a mathematical character. Even at this stage, however, it is difficult to resist the conclusion that the standard of rationality implied in the demand for strict sequentiality and seamless coherence of description is derived from ontological speculations to which the principle of causality gives expression. The indeterminacy principle has now turned the principle of causality into a superstition.[19] For the purpose of overall orientation the following table shows a range of philosophical and jurisprudential theses which bears on these matters. On a horizontal reading of the philosophical propositions in this table and considering their antithetical differences, one may well ask to what

---

[19] See Wittgenstein, *Tractatus Logico-Philosophicus* (London, 1922), 5.1361: "We cannot infer the events of the future from those of the present. Belief in the causal nexus is *superstition*." For a consideration of causality in a "realist" approach in the traditional meaning of this term (see *post* p. 59, n. 52) see the essay "Die Kausalitaet in der Natur" in Max Planck, *Vortraege und Erinnerungen*, 5th ed. (Stuttgart, 1951), p. 250.

extent each vertical arrangement sets out concordant comments on unwritten autobiographies.

Later on, standards of rationality will be considered and certain conclusions will follow. Together with those, which have so far been drawn, they will provide the orientations and re-orientations needed to disengage rules of procedure and evidence from doctrinal prejudice.

School		Empiricists, Utilitarians, Pragmatists, Positivists, Sociologists		Platonists, Idealists, Aquinists, Naturalists	Neo-Kantians, Rationalists (*Cogito ergo sum*)	Realists, Free Law School, Existentialists	
Subject		Philosophical	Jurisprudential	Philosophical	Jurisprudential	Philosophical	Jurisprudential
Teleology		The questions about the existence and knowledge of one's own self and that of another are meaningless.	The end of the law is to serve social interests.	The questions about the existence and knowledge of one's own self and that of another are meaningful.	The end of the law is the vindication of general principles.	The questions about the existence of one's own self and that of another are meaningless. The questions about the knowledge of one's own existence and that of another are meaningful.	The law has no end beyond the resolution of the individual legal conflicts.
Phenomenological Ontology		Relevant are only the correct formulation of issues and the physiological events in the sensory organs and nervous system. There is no psychical apperception.	The norm is a concretisation of prevailing social interests.	Inner and external perception are both psychical situations; both refer to ultimate factors.	The norm is a manifestation of a general principle.	Inner and external perception flow into each other; so do perceptive and non-perceptive situations; all situations can be ordered in meaningful structures.	The norm is the judicial or legislative rationalisation of decisions in previous cases.
Epistemology		Beyond logically formulated sentences and the physiological events in the nervous system there is no a priori cognition.	Social interests and their relation to individual desires are scientifically determinable.	Certain matters are known a priori.	Norms are definable and contexts can be delimited.	Certain matters are known a priori but there is no absolute a priori cognition as all a priori cognition is conditioned by life.	The concrete situation forms an original unit that cannot be dissected into norm and context.
Deontology		Truth or falsity (or several aspects of truth) are formal qualities of physical constructs. They are meaningful when they are controllable. There is no absolute truth.	The most correct decision protects the predominant social interests that are referable to the legal conflict.	Truth and falsity are qualities of non-physical constructs, called judgments; these are expressed in meaningful sentences. There is absolute truth.	The correct decision realizes the most important principle that is referable to the legal conflict.	Truth and falsity are qualities of all things; all what represents life is meaningful. There is no absolute truth.	The most correct decision can be found in the concrete situation in which the legal conflict arose.

CONTRADICTING

Previous inquiries have led to the descriptions of perceptual and recollective seriations and of the process of cumulation in circumstantial evidence; they were shown to be impervious to conceptual analysis on systematic-deductive lines. Hence a physicist may consider the "concept" of observation to be "elusive."[20] While these conditions are a challenge to the claim to pre-eminence of the conventional logical structure, the problems of negation and negative facts, which will now be considered, reach deeper; they disclose an inherent contrariety at the centre of this structure.

For the single person a fact-uncertainty is overcome internally, for instance when on the basis of circumstantial evidence a general forms an opinion on the likely state of affairs "on the other side of the hill." Typically, however, there is a dispute on the facts; it is dyadic in form, one side affirming a fact, the other contradicting. The basic tool of contradiction is negation, one side claiming that fact x exists, the other that it does not. In the terms of art of the rules of pleading one party "alleges" a fact, the other "traverses" it. Nothing could seem plainer than the symmetrical confrontation of affirmation and denial, and yet the search for the meaning of negative facts and of negation as such encounters a grave problem when this confrontation is viewed in terms of the opposition of existence and non-existence. To show the perennial character of the problem an early demonstration of the self-contradiction which here results is appended to these enquiries.[21] Through the intervening millenia this paradox of negation has remained unresolved; attempts to down-grade it or explain it away have failed. The advent of the computer as a logic machine has given a new importance to this problem.

Wittgenstein calls the problem "the mystery of negation. This is how things are, and yet we can say *how* things are *not.*"[22] Logic treats negation as a "logical constant" of an axiomatic character.[23] If, however, the notion of non-existence is indispensable to the attempt of understanding negation, then negation is not a simple, primitive notion and it would be arbitrary to treat it as an axiom. The problem arises as soon as the relation of the opposites of existence and non-existence is being considered for the fact of non-existence cannot be specified, except in terms of the thing which does not exist.[24] It is a necessary part of this

---

[20] G.E. Chew, "Bootstrap: A Scientific Idea?" (1968), 161 *Science*, 762, 765.
[21] Appx. A, *post* pp. 101-104.
[22] *Notebooks 1914-1916*, (Oxford, 1961), p. 30.
[23] G.F. Hughes and D.G. Londey, *The Elements of Formal Logic* (London, 1965), p. 150.
[24] *Cf.*, Appx. A, *post* p. 102 (67).

negative fact, and in view of this paradox it is not surprising that the law has vacillated in framing rules for the pleading of denials.[25]

Four fundamental conceptions are available for the attempt to gain an understanding of negation but none can avoid the paradox of negation, disclosing a self-contradiction.[26] These conceptions are: the conception of a negated proposition or possibility and the conceptions of opposition, difference and of non-being or non-existence. It will be found that the first three of these conceptions do not enable us to understand negation as such and that the fourth conception, while opening up a promising approach, establishes the ineradicable paradoxality of negation.[27]

In considering the propositional conception of negation let 'A' and 'B' stand for any two terms, 'r' for any relation between them, 'ArB' for any affirmative proposition and 'A not-r B' for the corresponding negation. The definition of 'A not-r B' is that 'ArB' does not apply to the facts. The words following the negative proposition are the definiens of the definition. The circumstance that the definiens, in trying to explicate negation, is invoking it shows the circularity of the definition. As 'ArB' stands for any specified relation, this is the case also for the negation 'A not-r B.' Yet as the definition of 'A not-r B' is that 'ArB' does not apply to the facts, the definiens achieves only the negation of the special relation of "applying to" and not the negation of the proposition 'ArB'.[28] If one tries to overcome this antinomy by first specifying the proposition negated and then denying that it applies to the facts, one obtains: " 'A is B applies to the facts' does not apply to the facts." But again this is a negation applying to a relation. It preserves the form of 'A not-r B' but it does not define the form of the negative fact which alone could make 'A not-r B' logically true, whereas this negative fact should by virtue of its form be capable of showing the fact that the proposition 'ArB' does not apply to the facts. This fact must then be the fact that " 'ArB' applies to the facts" does not apply to the facts. However, this process of trying to improve the definition can go on *ad infinitum* without eliminating the implied obscurity. This process cannot elucidate the meaning of a negation as such as each further step will once more point only to an infinite regress.

The same considerations apply if the negation of 'ArB' is conceived as the non-actualization of the possibility of 'ArB.' Here the fact that A has not r to B is the fact that the possibility 'ArB' is not actualized; but this

---

[25] See *post* pp. 74-5.
[26] Eric Toms, *Being, Negation and Logic* (Oxford, 1962), pp. 81-105.
[27] For the detailed argument on these four conceptions see *ibid.* pp. 81-95.
[28] The following comment by P.F. Strawson in his essay on truth, *supra*, n. 12: "What makes the statement 'the cat has mange' 'true' is not the cat but the *condition* of the cat, *i.e.*, the fact that it has mange" provides an example.

fact in turn is the fact that the possibility " 'ArB' is actualized" is not actualized, and so on.

As far as the conception of opposition is concerned, it indicates the incompatibility between two opposite propositions so that not both are true. It would then be necessary to show that the fact that not both p and q are true is the fact the proposition 'both p and q' are opposite to some true proposition 's'. If so, the issue becomes whether both 's' and 'both p and q' are true, and so on once more *ad infinitum*.[29]

The thesis that non-existence is not reducible to the conception of difference or otherness[30] is reinforced by Toms in a subsequent article[31] by means of the following argument:

Let a proposition be "It is a fact that Socrates is someone other than a sophist." In form this is a positive fact but it can be reduced to the negative fact "It is not a fact that Socrates is a sophist," as this is the equivalent of the first mentioned fact. Under the law of non-contradiction the opposite positive fact, namely "It is a fact that Socrates is a sophist," does not exist.[32] The equivalence of the first and the second facts shows that the first of these, while presupposing the conception of non-existence, hides this conception behind its apparently positive form. Hence by using only the conception of difference, an elucidation of the meaning of negation is not achieved and the only conception, which remains available for an understanding of negation is the conception of non-existence.

The conclusion that the conception of non-existence is indispensible to an understanding of negation is the penultimate step of the present argument.

Here we have turned once more to a Greek experience as the whole of this experience lies at the foundation of our way of life both as individuals and as communities, leaving its mark on our scientific outlook on nature and on our critical approach to it.[33] Gorgias pointed to the paradoxicality of the conception of non-existence by showing that the law of non-contradiction requires that the non-existence of something excludes its existence.[34] However, in the act of applying this law, "non-existence is re-introduced as an indispensible term of explanation."[35] As an account of non-existence can only be in terms of negation yielding a paradox and non-existence cannot be disassociated from negation, the paradox of non-existence spreads to the meaning of negation.

---

[29] *Supra*, n. 26, pp. 84-87.
[30] *Ibid.*, pp. 87-93.
[31] "The Problem of Negation" (1972), 15 *Logique et Analyse* (N.S.) 1.
[32] *Ibid.*, p. 8.
[33] See Z. Barbu, *Problems of Historical Psychology* (London, 1960), pp. 69 and 84 ss.
[34] Appx. A, *post* pp. 101-2, (66)-(71).
[35] *Supra*, n. 26, p. 92.

It is worthy of note that Gorgias characterizes "being" as *apeiron*. This adjective, due to the privative 'a,' has a negative meaning. It is usually translated as "unbounded" or "infinite." However, neither of these single terms can adequately present the polymorphous meanings of the original expression.[36] By attributing the quality of *apeiron* to "being," Gorgias, the agnostic par excellence, cannot avoid deifying it. The passage shows the force of religiosity breaking through a rationalization.

Plato's effort in the *Sophist*[37] to reduce the notion of non-existence to that of difference should not be considered as an attempt to refute the argument of Gorgias on the paradox of non-existence but to bypass it. In the *Sophist*, Gorgias is not mentioned by name but the dialogue contains sharp attacks on sophists in general, and Gorgias was widely considered their protagonist. Plato thought him sufficiently important to name an entire dialogue after him, and in this dialogue Gorgias is placed in a highly unfavourable light. Recently Plato's theory of negation, which has often been criticized, has found a new defender in Edward N. Lee.[38] Lee's defence of Plato rests on the argument that otherness constitutes non-being.[39] However, this can be so only if one subscribes to the Platonic theory of forms in which the categories of identity and otherness have the status of forms. Outside this theory otherness appears as a judgment of a relation between things rather than "constitutive" elements of the things themselves. As the platonic forms are unchanging and eternal whereas judging is typically a process of deliberation, Plato's theory of negation depends ultimately on treating "being" and "becoming" as incompatibles;[40] it seems more fruitful to consider "becoming" as the actualization of "being." Lee concedes that Plato's "account, then, will still involve a fundamental irreducible contrariety."[41] It would be different if negation was a simple term but it is not for only by reference to another term, that of affirmation,[42] is it

---

[36] Appx. A, *post* pp. 101-102 (69) 2 & 3 and (70) 5, translates the single Greek term *apeiron* by three negative adjectives; for a description of the semantic field of these terms and its history see Marcel Detienne et Jean-Pierre Vernant, *Les Ruses de l'Intelligence, La Mètis des Grecs* (Paris, 1974), pp. 269-285; for a general consideration of the problematics of *apeiron* in Greek speculative thought see H.B. Gottschalk, "Anaximander's Apeiron" (1965), 10 *Phronesis* p. 37, esp. p. 49.

[37] 255e-259b.

[38] "Plato on Negation and Not-Being in the Sophist," 81 *Philosophical Review* 267 at p. 298 n. 52, in this study Lee criticizes Toms for misinterpreting Plato's theory of negation; for an argument in depth which supports Toms' criticism of this theory see David Higgins, "Sentence Meaning, Negation and Plato's Problem of Non-Being," in *Plato, A Collection of Critical Essays*, Gregory Vlastos, ed. (Garden City, N.Y.), Vol. 1, pp. 298-302.

[39] Edward Lee, *ibid.*, n. 50.

[40] *Republic* Bk. VII 521D.

[41] See *supra*, n. 38, "Plato on Negation and Not-Being in the Sophist," at p. 298.

[42] *Cf.* Plato's reference to the unknowability of primary, this is to say simple elements in

possible to seek an understanding of non-existence and thus gain an insight into the problem of negation.

In his argument that the conception of non-existence is indispensible to negation for non-existence is not reducible to the other three fundamental conceptions Toms refers to a species which "exists" only in imagination, namely that of unicorns.[43] However, even in the more particular case of an imagined individual the infinite regress which negative statements develop will persist. To assert the non-being of the individual Pegasus is to deny his existence. Both statements are equivalent to the statements of the non-being of the being of Pegasus and, paradoxically so, also of the being of the non-being of Pegasus. This can be further extended to "the being of the non-being of the being of Pegasus" and so on *ad infinitum*.

This seriation shows further that the meaning of the statement "Pegasus does not exist" if far from being adequately brought out by pointing to the difference between Pegasus and existing things. The notion of difference is insufficient to reach the meaning of negation as such.

Plato seems to have been fully aware of this defect in his theory of negation and to be directly addressing himself to Gorgias when, in order to save the appearance of the rationality of the world, he wrote:

> And if someone mistrusts these apparent contradictions, he should study the question and produce some better explanation than we have now given; whereas if he imagines he has discovered an embarrassing puzzle and takes delight in reducing the arguments to a tug of war, he is wasting his time on a triviality, as our present argument declares. There is nothing clever in such discovery, nor is it hard to make; what is hard and at the same time worth the pains is something different.[44]

This type of criticism has persisted. Typically and interestingly so, it is scornful. This display of emotion discloses all too human feelings of insecurity and yearnings for certainty. One noted classicist went as far as to suggest that Gorgias wrote his book only in order to show off his ability to write in the philosophical vein.[45] This is a shrewd assessment of Gorgias' character, for Gorgias in his constant search for dramatic effects could not resist the temptation to use the paradox of non-existence for a *reductio ad absurdum* of the notion of existence. As criticism of Gorgias' work it is, however, excessive; it belittles his ability and genuine interest in philosophical and scientific questions which

---

Theaetus, 202E, and Wittgenstein's comments on this passage in *Philosophical Investigations* (Oxford, 1958), pp. 21-5.

[43] *Supra*, n. 26, pp. 89-90.

[44] *Sophist*, 259 B and C; the translation is by F.M. Cornford in his *Plato's Theory of Knowledge* (London, 1973), p. 297.

[45] Kathleen Freeman, *Pre-Socratic Philosophers* (Oxford, 1954), p. 362.

urged him to write his work. Today it can serve as a mark to gauge our progress or lack of it in resolving the paradox of non-existence.[46]

Returning to Plato's argument on the criterion of difference as explanation of negation, it is significant that historically his Academy was the first institute of higher learning in its several branches which was independent of religious establishments. This is not to say that Plato lacked reverence for religious observances, only that he offered a new vision. The Academy was founded at a time when the institution of sovereign city-states lost its viability and, concomitantly, the Olympic deities, who protected them, their ascendancy. At this juncture, critical minds were eager to endow philosophy with the authority which hitherto had belonged to the gods. The vision which Plato offered was different from that held out by established religion, in that it was not merely propitiatory but a vision of universal salvation in which emotion was uniquely blended with the reflection on it.

The last two words of his *Republic,* concluding his chapter on the immortality of the soul and the rewards of goodness, read in translation "we shall fare well," thus making a conditional prediction on man's ultimate destiny. In the original text, however, the verb is not in the future indicative to make a prediction but in the present subjunctive, expressing a hope. Hope rests on belief, and in view of the difficulty Plato experienced in determining the relation between the supercelestial and the mundane by means of the notion of "participation," he must have seen that belief was needed to subscribe to his transcendentalism. As the Greeks including Plato tried to make a clear distinction between belief and supposition on the one hand and knowledge on the other,[47] the virulence of Plato's attack on Gorgias can be understood as an overcompensation for the new uncertainties which are besetting philosophers once they complete the building of their abstract structures.

A similar situation obtains in modern times in which higher learning seeks to usurp the authority of religion. This learning increasingly models itself on natural science. The latter rests on theories which are algorithmically formulated, and many logicians consider it the task of logic to serve as the handmaiden of natural science. Hence they will experience an attack on the axioms of logic including that of negation not only as a threat to science but to reason itself and so to their own *raison d'être.* This may well explain the contemptuous tone which

---

[46] For an unbiased assessment of Gorgias' work see G.B. Kerferd, "Gorgias on Nature or That Which is Not" (1955), 1 *Phronesis* 3; it is regretted that the author considered it beyond the scope of his article to deal with "the question of how far the verb 'to be' can be used of phenomena without contradiction resulting." (*ibid.,* p. 23). G.E. Lloyd, *Polarity and Analogy* (Cambridge, 1971), p. 118 n. 1 seems to share Kerferd's view that Gorgias wrote a serious philosophical work; *cf.,* also *supra* p. 3.

[47] *Cf.,* Plato, *Gorgias* 454 d.

Williams[48] adopted in criticizing Toms' arguments. Williams described these as "effigies designed to hang themselves," thus taking up strictures which already Plato had voiced. Another critic, G.B. Keene[49] dismisses Toms as "a teacher of logic who wishes to abolish it," although his objective was to overcome the defects of "orthodox" logic.[50]

Yolton[51] acknowledges the importance of Toms' work. His main criticism is that Toms failed to distinguish between types of existence. This point was made already by Gorgias when he held that the "subsistence" of words should be distinguished from the "existence" of things.[52] Distinctions of the kind Yolton favours have lost much of their validity under the impact of sub-atomic particle theories which have led to an increasing etherealization or dematerialization of matter. Toms, in anticipation of Yolton's criticism, argues in his book that the distinction between types of existence is not tenable.[53] At the centre of Yolton's criticism are the perennial problems of the existential status of abstractions and of the relation between logic and ontology as it expresses itself in theories of universals and categories. Typically, abstractions emerge either in an "arrest" of experience before the experience becomes, as far as it is possible, commensurate with its source or by reflecting on a complete experience. The degree of generality of an abstraction will vary according to the interest in the experience. Every abstraction will reach however a degree of generalization even if no abstraction can be a mere abstraction. Hence the distinctions between types of existence made by Yolton lose much of their force.

A consideration of the general characteristics of a modern physical theory support this conclusion. A physical theory is a "contingently interpreted formalism disclosing a delicate trinity of algorithm, physical interpretation and correspondence rules."[54] These rules which according to the interpretation given to them prescribe the connection between theoretical terms and observed regularities are, however, systematic in character and therefore subject to Gödel's Theorem of Incompleteness.[55] As in science regularities are typically observed indirectly, the problem of cumulation, which arises in circumstantial

---

[48] See the review by Donald C. Williams in (1965), 74 *Philosophical Review* 390, 391-2 which mingles condescending praise with scathing criticism.
[49] In his review in (1963), 13 *Philosophical Quarterly* 277 whose main point seems to be that a logician has no business to talk metaphysics.
[50] *Ibid.*, p. 105.
[51] John W. Yolton, *Metaphysical Analysis* (Toronto, 1967), pp. 157, 162-4. Yolton, in contrast to Keene, seems surprised that Toms is so greatly exercised over nothing more than a problem of logic.
[52] Appx. A, pp. 103-104, (84) & (86).
[53] *Supra*, n. 26, pp. 17, 20, 25, 93, n. 1.
[54] N.R. Hanson, *The Concept of the Positron* (Cambridge, 1963), pp. 118-9.
[55] See *post*, p. 58.

evidence, appears also in physical theory. Again, an algorithm, however "broad" it may be,[56] is a logical structure. There the mystery of negation can make itself felt, for instance in theories of anti-matter. It is significant that Hanson expressly refers to the self-reflective paradoxes of logic and compares the "dematerialization of matter encountered in this century" to the intra-mathematical revolution brought about by Godel's theorem.[57] Toms considers these paradoxes to be "dwarfed" in importance by the paradox of negation.[58] The allergy of logic to self-contradiction has not prevented physicists from employing self-contradictory theoretical terms to explain particle-interaction. The "Bootstrap" model in sub-atomic theory, which takes its name from the expression "pulling oneself up by one's own bootstraps," is an example.[59] A main feature of this model is the self-contradictory hypothesis that certain sub-particles are "self-interacting" as they are "composites" of each other.[60] Not surprisingly, this notion is criticized for being "unscientific." Astrological predictions, for instance, are considered to be clearly unscientific although they are made by means of a logico-systematic method; however, a generally valid distinction between the scientific and the unscientific is most difficult, if not impossible to draw. At the other end of the spectrum natural science seeks to set itself off from the humanities by declaring the latter to be non-scientific as they are mainly concerned with interpretations which are unhampered by the stringency of "causal law." Even when the question of the validity of this law is being ignored, there remains the problem of interpretation. As mentioned, this problem plays an important role in physical theory so that the gap between scientific and non-scientific pursuits is much narrower than it is widely imagined to be.

At this point the objection has to be met that the imprecisions of physical theory, as exemplified by the Uncertainty Principle, apply in the microcosm but not in the macrocosm. This objection has lost much of its force. Not only are atomic reactors an important source of electrical energy but other applications of atomic theory and technology are on the increase.[61] As the scientific expert giving evidence on the event, which is in dispute, will typically be asked whether he has a theory supporting his opinion, the general frailty of a scientific theory, which manifests itself not only in physics but also, for instance, in

---

[56] *Supra*, n. 54 pp. 118 and 213 n. 2.
[57] *Ibid.* pp. 57 and 204 n. 4; see *post*, pp. 57 & 72 n. 23.
[58] *Supra*, n. 26, p. 122 n. 1.
[59] *Supra*, n. 20.
[60] *Ibid.*, p. 763.
[61] See *ibid.*, p. 765: "For example, the long-range Coulomb field underlies the existence of macroscopic solids from which measurement apparatus is constructed."

biochemistry, can no longer be overlooked in determining scientific and technological facts.

To gain an understanding of the role of science in human pursuits the metaphor of the spectrum was used. A more comprehensive view may be obtained by visualizing science as one segment of a circle. Astrology has been mentioned as an example of the unscientific; alternatively one may have chosen, for instance, the curative properties of certain remedies recommended by folk-medicine. Both have a strong connection with myth, and myth is parent to both poetry and philosophy; logic, a branch of the latter, is linked to science through the algorithms of scientific theory, thus closing the circle. These interrelations make it possible to view the paradoxes of logic as the penetrations of logic by a-logical elements which originate in other segments of the circle.

That formal logic ignores the problematic of its foundation can be seen in the propositional calculus. In this system a proposition is something that is either true or false. There is however a difference between the meaning of the term "proposition" and what is meant in a proposition so that the meaning of the verb "is" in "a proposition is something that . . ." has to be elucidated. Once more the problem of the meaning of '-p' arises. The proposition "The proposition '-p' is false" is a proposition '-p' about a proposition. Further, in proposition '-p' truth or falsity would be a predicate which as a term cannot be rigorously defined as a propositional element within the propositional calculus. It does not follow from the claim that propositions are either true or false that the propositions determine what is true or false.

This can be seen in the conjunction from which other logical constants can be derived. The conjunction 'p.q' is true or false if and only if 'p' and 'q' are true or false. This, however, does not amount to a determination of the symbol '.'. Usually the symbol stands for the expression 'and' but as Strawson[62] shows, this is far from being always the case. The use of the symbol '.' is here claimed to be valid by reason of the truth values of 'p' and of 'q'. This however is not a sufficient reason for the symbol to be able to transform the simple propositions 'p' and 'q' into the complex proposition that 'p.q' is true or false. To do so, the meaning of conjunction would have to be elucidated, and this formal logic does not do. It is concerned only with formal validity within an axiomatic system which presupposes meaning or legislates it, for instance regarding the effect of a double negation.

The transformation rules of logic intend to establish equivalences or symmetries between propositions. Negation, however, is no respecter of symmetries. There is equivalence between the proposition 'if A then B' and the proposition 'A does not hold without B holding.' If these two

---

[62] See n. 5, *Introduction to Logical Theory*, p. 80.

propositions are negated, one obtains for the first proposition 'A *can* hold without B holding' and for the second proposition 'A holds without B.' Hence the negation of the original propositions destroys their equivalence or symmetry and replaces it by an antinomy.

One will ask how formal logic is able to maintain its formidable authority although its foundations are so insecure. The answer is that the axiomatic structure of logic provides a system of order. This order expresses itself in the two-valued symmetries which the transformation rules of formal logic produce. But it should be clear that if the world is conceived as a manifestation of two-valued symmetries, as for instance in the mechanics of action and reaction, nothing new could ever happen, the same events would occur and re-occur. Hence two-valued logic looks for a mechanistic ontology, and it is only thanks to the logical paradoxes that there can be any hope of escaping from this stultifying world view. Further, conventional logic is "omnitemporal," it can turn its back to mundane existence and actual changes, it is a-historical. Plato could grant to the category of otherness the right of citizenship in his supercelestial realm as ostensibly it pays heed to the articulations of logic. He could not do the same for non-existence as then the logical structure of this realm would have been tainted by the paradox of negation.

There has been an unceasing quest to find in Nature the shadow or reflexion of a supercelestial, logical structure. Strivings which antedate those of Plato are here worthy of note. Heraclitus saw the clashes of antitheses hiding an ultimate *homologia*. Literally this term means "a speaking with the same voice" or univocality and it denotes a concord or *harmonia*. To describe this harmony he used a simile: "Harmony consists of opposing tensions like that of bow and lyre."[63] By using the bow as example Heraclitus points to the fact that the tension of the bowstring is the condition of the tension of the bow and the release of tension that of the flight of the arrow. It is significant that the bow is a man-made device. It can be considered as the prototype of a machine as the tension of the bow accumulates and stores energy for its release at will. This device both takes and preserves life; the loss of life of the prey is counterbalanced by the maintenance of the life of the hunter. Although the simile of Heraclitus is not wholly anthropocentric, the circumstances that he chose artifacts as examples of cosmic harmony remains highly significant. One may contrast this view with that of Gorgias. In perhaps the most important surviving thesis of his work Gorgias states that the language of the things is not our language.[64] The

---

[63] Fr. 51; translated by Kathleen Freeman, *Ancilla to the Pre-Socratic Philosophers* (Oxford, 1948), p. 46 from the emended text in Hermann Diels, *Die Fragmente der Vorsokratiker*, 11th ed. (Zurich, 1964), p. 162; see also Plato, *Republic* Bk. IV 439 b and c.

[64] Appx. A, p. 103 (84, lines 5-6).

voice of those things which are free from human intervention cannot be understood directly or completely; at best they offer themselves for interpretation, and our understanding is hampered by the equivocations in which interpretation results.[65] In Gorgias' view we cannot assert the *homologia* or harmony of the world for being can be described only negatively; it is *apeiron*, it will not release to us the secret of its being. It is a rejection of the thesis that what is being said by beings can properly represent what "being" says. And so Gorgias' work ends with the conclusion that truth in the classical sense of *adaequatio rei et intellectus* is inaccessible to our logic.

The foregoing inquiries were intended to show that a logic without an ontology is an impossibility. But the question is whether an ontology free of circular postulates is a possibility. The criticisms levelled against monistic and dualistic ontologies alike have led to the hypostasis of an unlimited number of possible worlds. However, the general problem of infinity combines here with specific problems encountered by modal logic so as to leave a logically founded ontology only a remote hope.[66] It is one thing to sail in exploration over uncharted depths, it is another to ignore their reefs.

Before dealing with the consequences which the foregoing inquiries have for the manner of taking expert evidence, the historical and social dimensions which are here involved have to be considered. Only then will it be possible to gain an adequate understanding of the deep-rooted reasons for the reluctance to put into practice a measure of reform which on its face has much to commend itself.

---

[65] *Supra*, n. 54, Ch. V, pp. 71-92.
[66] For recent developments in modal and tense logic see the postscript by Kit Fine to A.N. Prior's posthumously published *World, Time and Selves* (London, 1977), pp. 138, 153-8.

Chapter 4

Superstructures

INTERPENETRATIONS OF PUBLIC AND PRIVATE LAW ELEMENTS

Interpenetrations between elements of a whole presuppose their difference. It is easier to see a distinction between private and public acts than between the rules which address themselves to these modes of behaviour. In the common law, especially, it is one thing to acknowledge the general validity of the distinction, it is another to find a reliable criterion for it. It is different in those civil law jurisdictions where the administration of a coherent body of certain laws, generally considered to be preponderately public in character, has for long been the exclusive province of a hierarchy of tribunals which function independently of the ordinary courts.[1]

In Rome, language made the distinction between public and private fields of behaviour ostensive. The former involved the people as a whole, the latter had the negative meaning of that which was not public. The expressions "deprived" and "privative" retain this meaning. Common to all and therefore public was the city state, the typical form of urban settlement on the Mediterranean littoral. In Greek political theory, the city was an autonomous whole which fully encompassed its members. In the praise of *philotimia*, the love of honour, the existence of the citizen as an entity of its own was acknowledged but the polis represented a higher form of existence.[2] Its laws reflected a cosmic order which set the standards of human justice. The Greek idea of the state as an entity governed by law was reached in this specific way.[3] Transformed much later into absolutist terms, "the state in and by itself is the ethical whole.... The basis of the state is the power of reason actualizing itself as will".[4] This construction linked cosmology, sociality and law into a coherent view of the appearance of the human world.

Pragmatically, the Romans centred their attention on human law, not on cosmology. Basic to their jurisprudence was the notion of the *persona* as bearer of rights and duties. This notion had sufficient

---

[1] See A.V. Dicey, "Droit Administratif in French Law" (1907), *L.Q.R.* 302; "The Development of Administrative Law in England" (1915), 31 *L.Q.R.* 148.
[2] "... stateless the man who dares to dwell with dishonour" Sophocles, *Antigone*, 370-1.
[3] Otto von Gierke, *Das Deutsche Genossenschaftsrecht*, Vol. III (Graz, 1954), pp. 8-34, 186-208.
[4] Hegel, *Philosophy of Right* (Oxford, 1952), p. 279.

generality to apply both to the relation of the citizen with the *res publica* or republic and with his neighbours. Pre-eminent was the *persona* of the *pater familias* who by inheritance held dominium over his household. It included the *patria potestas*, the power of life and death even over adult sons. In the context of patriarchy it is of interest that in the records of the Sumerians, a society as patriarchal as that of Rome, the notion of freedom was expressed by a phrase which in literal translation means "return to the mother."[5] In the transactions of the fully qualified citizen with other heads of households, Roman law provided the first demarcation of private from public law.

Athens was a republic of burgesses, Rome a republic of families. Hence, there were marked differences between them in regard to the distribution of co-operative and egocentric elements in the constitution of the group and the status of its members. These differences showed themselves also in warfare, "the father of all things."[6] The Greek soldier was a pikeman fighting in a serried column of close-packed shields. Each depended on the strictest co-operation of the others, and he surrendered his initiative to the group. The Roman soldier was a swordman fighting in line. The battle order was more extended, and in close combat the Roman relied on himself and his nearest comrades, not on the cohesion of the group.

The formal dichotomy into public and private law was performed by the Glossators of the 12th century A.D. They provided a theoretical basis for the legal continuity of the group regardless of changes in its membership. In this context, general terms for the legal relations between group and singular persons were established. Gradually, these terms replaced the ample particularizations characteristic of earlier times. Normative terms took the place of descriptions. In the civil law this fruit of scholastic labour resulted early in the equivalence of singular and corporate entities as legal personalities. The common law refused to follow suit. There, the doctrine of *ultra vires* preserved the older method of particularizing the scope of corporate status. This doctrine overrides the distinction between public and private law.

Belatedly, pragmatically, common-law jurisdictions developed a modern administrative law of their own. Two major influences gave the common-law jurisdictions their specific character. The doctrines of Locke, which provided a theoretical basis for the Great Settlement of 1689, and the factory system which became the paradigm of productive organization are the landmarks. These influences, which originally diverged only to converge in the end, shaped the colonization of North America where most settlements began as towns and not as villages.

---

[5] Samuel N. Kramer, *The Sumerians* (Chicago, 1963) p. 79; Sumerian is the oldest script of which specimens have survived.

[6] Heraclitus, fr. 53, and *supra*, p. 40 n. 63.

With the Great Settlement passed the mediaeval attitude that expected the king "to live of his own." It meant that, at least in times of peace, the cost of public administration was to be borne by the patrimony of the ruler, that is the Crown lands directly held by him, his feudal reservations of rent and his financial shares in monopolies and trading ventures. The taxes which were levied by act of parliament were called "subsidies." They were raised mainly for emergencies. Accordingly, the civil law concept of the fisc as the legal holder of the entire property of the state and its income gained ground only slowly. Even the abolition of first the judicial and later the administrative functions of the sheriff and their transfer to justices of the peace did not result in a systematic development of an administrative law in the civil-law sense of the term. The Anglo-Norman aim of a law common to all, administered by courts of general jurisdiction, was not given up easily. The increase in administrative autonomy of cities and boroughs arrested rather than furthered a systematic development of a common administrative law. Typically, these entities had received confirmations and enlargements of their charters not by a constitutional process but by particular bargains made with the Crown.

The charter as instrument of a grant or confirmation of particular rights and duties was used also by guilds and trading companies thus blurring the distinction between public and private law elements. The aim of English administrative law is a justice which is considered "natural," and its case law describes the variations on this theme. When a new technology had reinforced the process of urbanization, thus increasing physical interdependence, the individualistic doctrines of the Great Settlement prevented measures of general welfare from keeping abreast of its tasks. In this evolution, the problematics of group personality, group decision, group structure and group belief were once more put to the test. In the law, this manifested itself in their justifications of the notion of group personality. These oscillate between a group based on contract and having an "organic" character, and the construct of a fiction. In his *Second Treatise of Government,* Locke relied on the notion of a Social Contract.[7] Employing this language, the resolution of the House of Commons of the Convention Parliament of 1689 stated:

> That King James II, having endeavoured to subvert the constitution of his kingdom by breaking the original contract between king and people . . .[8]

It was left to Rousseau to base his "General Will" and the foundations of

---

[7] Sections 95 ss.
[8] See Cobbett's *Parliamentary History of England* (London, 1809), Vol. V, p. 50; this wording is quoted also by Taswell-Langmead, *English Constitutional History,* 10th ed. (London, 1946), pp. 498-9, citing *Commons Journal* X 14, 15.

a legal order on Locke's social contract. The constitution of the United States represents a further development of this amalgam of doctrines.

This outline of exercises of the imagination which have made history suggests that descriptions of diachronic and synchronic changes are likely to offer a more favourable route for the discovery of the distinction between public and private law. For this approach, a frame of reference is needed. The diagram[9] shown on the following page is a frame of this kind. It provides means of orientation in the search for meanings of actual states of affairs and their changes. The diagram is a two-dimensional, bounded model. As the border of something is always one dimension behind the thing itself, the lines of the diagram indicate boundary conditions of structures and beliefs. These conditions are determined jointly by the fields which are bordered by the lines. Lines establish dualities and these, in turn are mediated by the lines. In this way, the meanings of the descriptions shown in the several fields of the diagram mutually support each other. Hence, the diagram points to transitional coherences and thus to compatibilities as well as to contraries and negations, giving unity to the diagram as a whole. The group line which dissects the diagram horizontally denotes the experience of social bonds, the vertical grid line the experience of social stratifications. Arrows protrude from these two lines to indicate the possibilities of changes of time and changes in time.

Each square of the diagram shows a social and a legal structure linked to a pattern of belief. Together they form distinct profiles. While not claiming to describe actual appearances, they provide topics for a relevant description of actual states of affairs. Being a model, the diagram can describe its own zero condition. This condition of lack of belief and structure is shown at the centre of the diagram. The group and grid lines do not cross the zero mark. It indicates that the mark should be read as a point, a thing without borders.

---

[9] The diagram is derived from those in Mary Douglas, *Natural Symbols* (London, 1970), pp. 59-60, 103-105, 141-143; see also G.H. Kendal, "The Role of Concepts in the Legal Process" (April, 1962), 1 *U.B.C.L.R.* 642.

Interpenetrations of Public and Private Law Elements   47

GROUP

PROFILES

	C. REGULATIVE	D. PROGRAMMATIC	
COSMOLOGY	"Men are the masters and possessors of Nature" (Descartes). The world manifests itself in regulative combinations of dangerous and benign elements.	The world is divided between warring forces of good and evil. The duality of the world is overcome in victory or in defeat.	**COSMOLOGY**
SOCIAL	Singular and group purposes are reconciled. Behaviour is ritualistic and addresses itself to both group cohesion and the protection of status.	Group membership is the only relevant status.	**SOCIAL**
LEGAL	Rules balance private rights and public responsibilities, private duties and civic rights.	Private rights and duties are subordinated to group rights and duties.	**LEGAL**

GRID ←   O

STRUCTURES

	LEGAL	Rules secure the priority of private rights and duties.	Rules and sanctions are minimized.	**LEGAL**	
	SOCIAL	Each singular person relates to others in categories focussed on himself. Behaviour is manipulative, subgroups are ephemeral.	Roles and symbols are ambiguous, leadership precarious. Perverted or defective humans are the main danger. Groups respond to it by withdrawals.	**SOCIAL**	
	COSMOLOGY	Men are the possessors of Nature. Private magic is used to secure success. Expectations are millenarian.	Nature is benign, religion personal, the will irrelevant.	**COSMOLOGY**	

A. MANIPULATIVE	B. LIBERTARIAN

PROFILES

The profiles of the diagram differ in their temporal perspective. In profile A past and future dominate the present, in profile B the present dominates past and future and in profile D the future dominates past and present. Only in profile C do past, present and future appear as equivalent. The balance, in the sense of compatibility of functional elements, stipulated in profile C serves as a standard against which the variations of cooperation and egocentricity shown in the other squares of the diagram can be gauged.

The foregoing descriptions provide a plurality of cosmological resonances. In the formalization of the dichotomy of the law into a public and a private segment, the civil law had the equivalence expressed by profile C as its aim. The common law refused to equate formalization with realization. Yet, the dichotomy gives expression to the primordial polarity of group and singular person. Criminal law puts this polarity into relief. Administrative law uses some of the sanctions of the criminal law. This brings it closer to criminal law than to contract or property law. The demarcation line between criminal and administrative law is blurred, and Glanville Williams could establish no better criterion than to find a rule to belong to the criminal law when it is applied in a criminal court.[10]

It is conceded that, in the abstract, rules of criminal and administrative law appear as impositions but that in contract the parties appear to legislate for themselves. Yet, in plea bargaining or negotiating the terms of a probation order or suspended sentence, consent plays an important role. On the other hand, consent is affected when a party was unable to negotiate the terms of a warranty or even any of the terms of a contract. Situations in which the notion of imposition proclaims unambiguously the public or private character of a legal relation are not representative.

However, the notion of imposition provides clues which make a distinction between the public and private elements in a legal relation possible. This is the directness or indirectness of the transaction involved. The prototype of transactional directness is the mode of subsistence of animals who grasp and consume their food in a single transaction. For men, production, processing, transportation, storage and cooking intervene. As long as things are produced only for a consumption which makes further production possible, the production-consumption chain is circular, and the experience of subsistence retains much of its direct character. By producing surpluses, the chain becomes a spiral. This added dimension renders the experience of subsistence indirect. Legal institutions formalize the relations between the elements of the production-consumption chain.

---

[10] Glanville L. Williams, "The Definition of Crime" (1955), 8 *Curr. Leg. Problems* 107; *McNeill v. A.G. of Nova Scotia* (1976), 14 N.S.R. (2d) 225 at pp. 228 and 247 (C.A.).

The notion of directness should not be expected to provide an infallible criterion for the distinction between public and private law elements. It has however sufficient discriminatory strength to express distinct experiences of the legal process and thus to provide core meanings for the terms public law and private law, respectively. The criminal act is seen as a direct interference with the "peace" of the group. In the wider sense of the term a criminal act is a transaction. The penal reaction is its counterpart. This reaction tends towards the same degree of directness which is characteristic of the criminal act. It cannot reach it however as the surroundings in which adjudication functions will mitigate, typically, the *lex talionis*.[11] Even so, the penal reaction will display sufficient directness to compete with self-help, of which blood-feud is the prime example. Hence, in criminal law and by derivation in administrative law, manifestations of direct transactionality will be more prominent than in property or contract law.

The latter offers a favourable point of observation for the tendency towards indirectness of the private law. The common law, as it is developed first, concentrated its effort on the provision of a uniform administration of justice in areas of strategic importance to the social structure. Accordingly, the pre-existing, internationally oriented mercantile law whose rules were designed to serve overseas trade, was for long left intact. The indirect character of these commercial transactions is reflected in the negotiability of its bills of exchange and lading and, in particular, in its monetary sanctions and bankruptcy laws. In contrast stands the bond, an institution of the common law, whose sanctions of forfeiture and imprisonment gave these transactions a direct character.

Elsewhere, especially in the universities of Northern Italy, a systematization of contract law was begun. It provided the degree of generality and abstraction needed for the executory contracts of sale of a newly expanding international trade. The civilian definitions of contractual relations which were developed for this purpose became a model for other private law relations.

In its sophisticated forms in France and Germany the articulations of contract law moved with a drill-like precision. Its absence in the common law cannot be accounted for only by the contingencies of the intervention of equity. Sale of Goods statutes of the English type consisted largely of the enumeration of rules which prudent and diligent parties had used as standards of commercial conduct since time immemorial. No legislative need was felt to achieve complete consistency for the operational concepts of these statutes or to align

---

[11] *I.e.*, the law of retaliation.

them thoroughly to the law of chattels.[12] For transactions in which the laws of contract and of property interact, public registers were established and these modern statutes contain mandatory provisions. The deep-rooted resistance of the common law to legislative systematizations of contract law places it in contrast not only to the internal consistency of the provisions on the sale of goods in the German Civil Code but also to the overall consistency between these provisions and those of the General Part of the Code, where the laws of contract and of property are coordinated systematically. One should however recall here that in the heydays of contract law, this is to say before the times of modern vertical and horizontal oligopolies and consumer protection legislation, no court enjoyed a higher reputation than the Commercial Court of the High Court of England.

Trading requires the privacy of the counting house as well as the publicity of the marketplace. Coincident with the predominance of contractual relations, a consequence of the Great Settlement, was the demand for greater personal privacy. The layout of dwellings began to meet this demand. Sets of intercommunicating rooms with only a single door to the outside gave way to an arrangement in which each room had its own access door. Similarly, the communal meal for which all food was placed together on the tables of the common hall was transformed into a sequence of courses served in a dining room. From an evolutionary point of view there is a certain incongruity in the boundary case of this development. The single diner taking his meal in a private room is returning to the solitude in which many vertebrates take and consume their food. This behaviour is antithetical to the sociality inherent in the cooperative efforts which provided the food.[13] In line with growing individualist, egocentric tendencies the experience of sustenance acquired an indirect character.

These tendencies were reinforced by the Great Settlement;[14] they strengthened the indirect character of contract law. Its governing theme, *pacta servanda sunt*, was left without direct sanctions when damages replaced forfeitures and imprisonment for debt. Specific performance became a rare exception. If the contract concerned fungibles, the parties were referred to commodity markets. There, the direct duty of keeping one's word, a salient element of sociality, became submerged in covering transactions. Tocqueville foresaw the deepening of human solitude as the consequence of these tendencies.[15] The general

---

[12] See P.S. Atiyah, *The Sale of Goods* (London, 1957), pp. 141, 143 and 145; in its central meaning "chattel" refers to movable property.
[13] *Cf.*, Glynn Isaac, "The Food-sharing Behaviour of Protohuman Hominids" (April, 1978) *Scientific American*, 90.
[14] Even appointments in the public service and army promotions were bought and sold.
[15] *Democracy in America*, tr. (New York, 1945), Vol. II, pp. 98-101 and 228.

provisions of the Municipal Corporations Act[16] which safeguard minimum conditions of urban co-existence may be considered the starting point of modern administrative law in common law jurisdiction. In the realization of its aim, this body of laws and the public enterprises which are subject to it encountered a fully articulated body of private law whose transactions and sanctions had become increasingly indirect.

The interventionist character of the modern state is most visible in modern public enterprises.[17] In form, they may range from semi-autonomous branches of government departments, government-owned institutes, boards of commissioners, Crown corporations to ordinary limited companies. Some may have purely administrative, supervisory, research, or information functions, others are carriers, manufacturers or traders. These intermesh in their transactions with private enterprises pursuing private ends. In this sense private law elements penetrate into the sphere of public law, though perhaps not to the same degree to which public law elements penetrate private law relations.

Mixed enterprises represent a further step in the intervention of the state in economic activities. In these cases, which are becoming more frequent,[18] both sides commit themselves directly to the success of the enterprise. There is, however, an inherent conflict on what should be considered a success. The participation by the state is the realization of a public policy, for instance regarding employment, energy, environment or defence, whereas the overall aim of the business sector is a reasonable level of profitability.[19] A certain reconciliation of these aims may have been achieved when the terms of the participation were agreed upon. It does not follow however that these general understandings are adequate to resolve differences of opinion on the actual conduct of the affairs of the enterprise.

In these situations, the heterogeneous character of the laws which

---

[16] 5 and 6 Will. 4 c. 76.

[17] For the story of the new interventions of public law see Stone, *Social Dimensions of Law and Justice* (London, 1966), Ch. 5, especially the literature cited on pp. 253-4, n. 232 and Ch. 3, para. 8; on governmental enterprises see C.D. Drake, "The Public Corporation as an Organ of Government Policy," pp. 44-5; J.E. Hodgetts, "The Public Corporation in Canada," pp. 206-26; W. Friedmann, "Government Enterprise: A Comparative Analysis," pp. 303-6, in *Government Enterprise* (London, 1970), W.G. Friedmann and J.F. Garner, eds. and see Andrée Martin-Pannetier, *Elements D'Analyse Comparative des Etablissements Publics en Droit Français et en Droit Anglais* (Paris, 1966), pp. 23-30, 122-6, 188-226 and 318-341.

[18] S.D. Clark, *The Developing Canadian Community*, 2nd ed. (Toronto, 1968), pp. 232-248; cf., W.L. Mackenzie King, *Industry and Humanity*, 2nd ed. (Toronto, 1973), pp. 262 ss.

[19] According to Max Weber, *The Protestant Ethic and the Spirit of Capitalism* (New York, 1958), pp. 47-8, 162; this spirit appears to be a particular blend of rationality and restraint.

legitimize the mixed enterprise makes itself felt. The legal authorization for the participation by the state may be an enabling or constitutive statute which displays the public policy involved, whereas the private partner is relying on the general laws governing business investments, and these belong mainly to the area of private law. Paradoxical situations may develop. In a matter of dividend policy, for instance, one faction on the board of directors may favour a liberal course, another the accumulation of reserves. In the ensuing litigation, the objectives of the state participation in the enterprise may come under judicial review, but the primary frame of reference under which the review is being conducted may be a Companies Act that institutionalizes private means and ends. This intertwinement of public and private law elements will make new demands on the fact-finding task in which explanations for the contested decision of the board of directors are being sought. The issues of interpretation and evidence which are here involved may reach a high level of complexity if the modes of production, the quality or the price of the goods or services produced by the mixed enterprise are subject to regulation.

Decisions of the kind considered here are not made by a singular person but by a group, for instance a board of directors or commissioners, and their decision itself is an act. Only rarely will these decisions have the simple meaning of "the door is to be opened, closed, kept open or closed." The meaning of a group decision depends largely on the explanation which can plausibly be given for it. A presumption of intention in terms of ostensive means and ends or compliance with a declared policy will be inadequate to explain the decision if the group consists of heterogeneous elements and consensus was reached by an accommodation of overlapping or conflicting interests. Adequate explanations for decisions of this kind can be obtained only by a more demanding fact-finding task than that of the traditional civil or criminal process.

The outcome of a review of a group decision depends on the explanations which can be found for it, and their plausibility issues from the relevant facts of the case. These facts are of two kinds which are interconnected in various degrees. There is the external situation with which the group was faced. This situation includes the anticipated reactions of other groups to the alternatives which are being considered. There are further the internal factors of the decision-making process. Without taking these into consideration, explanations of a group decision will be misleading, and the review of a group decision be distorted. Expectations of the behaviour of others oscillate between the beliefs that people will continue to act in the same way in which they had acted before and that they will behave rationally or reasonably. Rationality directly invokes logicality, reasonableness first appeals to sociality. The margin of difference between rationality and reasonableness will be enlarged by those who are willing to overlook the inherent limitations of logic and the inconclusiveness of tensed predicate logic[20] while those who emphasize these limitations will tend to assimilate rationality to reasonableness.

On the whole, the notion preferred by the law is that of "reasonableness." In many fields, it is the ultimate criterion of approved conduct.[21] However, its reification in the model of the "reasonable man" encourages circular reasoning, a blemish which legal logic condones more easily than practical reasoning. In some disputes it can be argued with equal plausibility that liability hinges on the reasonableness of the impugned conduct and that the question of reasonableness is answered by the liability it attracts. The defects of the notion of rationality are less obvious but equally grave. This notion is confronted with the persistent doubt whether language is logic or logic linguistic. In mathematics this doubt reappears as the uncertainty whether its rules are conventions or the manifestations of a cosmic order.[22] Hence the search for reliable criteria and methods of rational behaviour continues. At present, the *maximin* and the *minimax* principles[23] which are designed to permit the calculation of maximum gains and minimum losses respectively in a given situation, enjoy a considerable prestige. However, from the practical point of view, the minimax calculus can be criticized for encouraging overcautious attitudes by concentrating too much attention on the "worst case" of a contingency.[24] Moreover both calculuses can operate only in systematized fields so that they share the inability of important systems to be both complete and consistent.

The lowest common denominator of the criticisms which can be levied against the conventional notion of rationality is its insufficiency as explanation of a decision. On the other hand, the seeming simplicity of this notion with its straight line interconnections between the elements of a decision-making process favours the building of a model of rational

---

[20] See Arthur Prior, *Past, Present and Future* (Oxford, 1967), p. 174.
[21] See in *Re Polemis*, [1921] 3 K.B. 560 at pp. 569-70 (C.A.) on "reasonable foreseeability"; on the reasonableness of a belief as evidence of good faith see *Liversidge v. Anderson*, [1942] A.C. 207 at 220; for an overview see A. Harari, *The Place of Negligence in the Law of Torts*, (Melbourne 1962), pp. 120 ss, 168-79; R.E. Samek, "Some Reflections on the Logical Basis of Mistake of Identity of Party" (1960), 38 *Can. Bar Rev.* 479 at pp. 507-8; R. Powell, "The Unreasonableness of the Reasonable Man" (1957), 10 *Current Legal Problems* 104.
[22] *Cf.*, G.H. Kendal, "Computing Limits of Time" (April, 1967), *Canadian Bar Journal* 117 at pp. 122-3.
[23] For the formalization of the "minimax" idea into a theorem see Maurice Frechet, "Commentary on Three Notes of Emile Borel" (Jan., 1953), 21 *Econometrica* 118 - 124 and J. von Neuman, "Communication on the Borel Notes," *ibid.*, pp. 124-5; see also Herbert Simon, "A Behavioural Model for Rational Choice" (1955), 69 *Quarterly Journal for Economics* 99 and 113-14.
[24] For a demonstration of the minimax calculus see Thomas C. Schelling, *The Strategy of Conflict* (New York, 1963), pp. 46-52.

behaviour. A recent study shows the shortcomings of this model and supplements it with two others.[25] These three models are labelled "rational actor," "organizational process" and "government politics" model, respectively. Although the study takes the Cuban missile crisis of 1962 as its subject, the two last-mentioned models provide, *mutatis mutandis,* frameworks also for explanations of decisions outside the field of foreign policy.

The three models mentioned differ in their governing themes, establish different topics and point to different relevances. The main explanatory features of the "rational actor" model are the objectives of a decision in terms of a rational choice of actions and consequences. In the "organizational process" model, the decision which is being scrutinized is considered as output of the organization. This output is preformed by the standard operating procedures, programmes and repertoires of the organization. Decision is preceded by departmentalized, problem-directed research which is centrally co-ordinated and controlled. The goals of the action are constrained by established standards of acceptable performance. The "government politics" model makes a further contribution to the explanation of a group decision. In this model, goals and action channels are determined by the "stakes" and "stands" of the several actors who are engaged in a competitive power play. The decision itself is considered as the resultant of a bargaining process.

These different models for the explanation of a group decision have different effects on the relevance of the evidence which is adduced in support of an explanation of the decision. For the "rational actor" model, evidence of the behaviour of the actors will be "marshalled in such a way that a coherent picture of the value-maximizing choice from the point of view of the [group] emerges." This requires "rules of evidence for making assertions about objectives, options and consequences that permit the [review] to distinguish among the various accounts."[26] In using the "organizational process" model, relevance centres on information concerning organization, routines and standard operating procedures of the group and their changes. For the "government politics" model, which applies to public and private institutions alike, the main difficulty may be the accessibility of evidential material. Documentary evidence on bargaining, accommodations or compromises within a group or between groups may show gaps or will not be available at all. The evidence will then often consist of conflicting testimony.[27]

---

[25] Graham T. Allison, *Essence of Decision* (Boston, 1971), pp. 10-14, 67-96 and 144-181.
[26] *Ibid.,* p. 35.
[27] *Ibid.,* pp. 86 and 180.

The last quotation[28] called for rules of evidence in the use of the "rational actor" model. These rules affect the admissibility of a "decision tree," which is a schematic presentation of alternative courses of action and consequences and forms part of an explanation of the decision under review. From a legal point of view there should be little objection to a presentation of this kind. It is another matter to make decision procedures, which are modelled on those of the propositional calculus of formal logic, binding upon the reviewer as an incontestable standard of rationality. This qualification may be of decisive importance in the concrete case as the structure of the information retrieval system, from which the "decision tree" is derived, may give one of the parties a large measure of control over the availability of particular items of evidence. The imbalance in information is likely to increase when the "organizational process" and "government politics" models are used. Appropriate rules of evidence can provide remedies for this imbalance.

The indeterminate aspects of the "rational actor" model can in many cases be ignored. Further, this model claims a wider scope than the other two models as it seeks to serve both the decision of a singular person and that of a group. On the other hand, the "organizational process" model, in assimilating the behaviour of a decision-making group to that of factory operatives producing an output, has an hyperbolic character. Again, the "government politics" model invites us to go backstage where not only disillusion but also confusion may wait. These shortcomings explain in part the ability of the "rational actor" model to survive in the face of frequent criticism. A further scrutiny of the justifications and limitations of the notion of rationality and of its role in decision making is needed.

MACHINE-REGULATED BEHAVIOUR

In a debate on artificial intelligence a computer scientist claimed that "nothing" should be the answer to the question "What do judges know that we cannot tell a computer?".[29]

To tell something to a computer, one programmes it. A programme is a set of instructions which provides a procedure for the solution of a problem. The procedure processes information according to established transformation rules into a language acceptable to a machine. In one perspective, decision making is an operation in which information is being processed. This aspect forms the basis for the claims of a potential equivalence between artificial and natural intelligence.

The main feature of the computer is neither the speed of its operations

---

[28] *Ibid.*, p. 65.
[29] Joseph Weizenbaum, *Computer Power and Human Reason* (San Francisco, 1976), p. 207.

nor its memory-holding capacity but that it mechanizes language. Every state the computer attains is completely described by symbols which automatically convey instructions for further operations. Although only the two symbols '0' and '1' are needed to make the machine obey instructions, they provide vocabulary and grammar for a language which describes the rules of behaviour of the machine.[30]

The meaning of each of these symbols has a high degree of precision. The contrast with the plasticity of natural language could not be greater. Yet, the paradox of non-existence which is implicit in the relation of the symbols '0' and '1', generates the further paradox of negation. It points to uncertainties[31] in computer operations which at first sight are hidden by the binary "flip-flop" arrangements of the computer gates.

Computer language is considered "a formal or logical (or mathematical) system."[32] The first of these three attributes evokes a doctrine in which forms embody the principle of an ascending rationality. In attributing logicality to a system, one asserts its consistency and the power of a formal language[33] to demonstrate this consistency. Calling a system mathematical, the enumerability and computability of the system elements are stressed. These characteristics refer back to the formal and logical features of a system. In this triad of attributes, logicality holds the key position; it is claimed to be the touchstone of rationality.

As discipline, logic shades almost imperceptibly into others. At its core there are two elementary methods, the inclusionary method and the combinatorial. They are indispensable in computer operations. In the former method two terms are posited and these are linked by a middle term. This term can show its probative value in two ways: If the middle term is included in the first term and includes the second term, the latter can be included in the first term. This operation provides a taxonomy with its extensional order. Validity depends ultimately on the counter-intuitive axiom that there are classes without members.[34]

In the other branch of the inclusionary method the middle term is included in the second term and includes the first. The first term can then be included in the second. Here, the middle term is more than an

---

[30] *Ibid.*, pp. 60-61.
[31] See *supra* pp. 31 ss.
[32] Marvin L. Minsky, *Computation: Finite and Infinite Machines* (Englewood Cliffs, N.J., 1967), pp. 219-20.
[33] *I.e.*, a logical language which satisfies "the conditions, that every expression grammatically well constructed as a proper name out of signs shall in fact designate an object, and that no new sign shall be introduced as a proper name without being secured as a reference." *Translations from the Philosophical Writings of Gottlob Frege*, Peter Geach and Max Black, eds. (Oxford, 1952), p. 70.
[34] See Harold Newton Lee, *Symbolic Logic* (New York, 1961), pp. 87, 88 and 97.

intermediary link, it gives a reason for the inclusion. Between them the two versions of the inclusionary method provide the definitions and consistencies of systemic order. However, neither operation yields adequate descriptions of change as only rates of change can be given, not qualitative differences.

The second method is combinatorial. Here, instead of aiming from the general at the particular, the relation between the simple and the complex is scrutinized in order to criticize the definitions which the inclusionary method provides. Two strategies are available for this operation. In a synthesis, which starts with the simple, concepts are formed. However, to validate this strategy a principle is needed capable of determining why one systemic set of concepts is superior to others which could be constructed also. The strategy of analysis offers better prospects. It proceeds by reducing first the more complex to the more simple. The search is for primitive terms, for the indecomposable elements of a complex, and for the pattern of their interrelations.[35] One expects to arrive at a set of knowable facts which can be isolated from the other elements of the complex[36] and represented systematically.

As procedure, analysis culminates in an assembly operation. It is eminently suitable for mathematics and for physics also wherever the methodology of this discipline is being assimilated to that of mathematics.[37] The price which is being exacted for the disambiguations[38] which are being achieved is value-ascesis.

It might be a price worth paying, were the loss of value compensated by a decisive gain in certainty. Gödel's theorem[39] shows that this is not the case. This theorem holds that "every interesting formal system has some statements whose truth or falsity cannot be decided by the formal means of the system itself, in other words, that mathematics must necessarily be forever incomplete."[40] Further, "for the more important, wider systems, completeness implies contradiction as in such a system, at least one true proposition is found such that, if it is provable within that system, a contradiction is incurred."[41] In consequence, if such system asserts its own consistency, it will be incomplete. It is a

---

[35] Louis Lavelle, *Manuel de la Méthodologie Dialectique* (Paris, 1962), p. 80.
[36] See James K. Feibleman, *Inside the Great Mirror* (The Hague, 1961), p. 183.
[37] *Cf., supra* p. 1 and *post* p. 85 n. 60.
[38] *I.e.*, the removal of ambiguities.
[39] See Ernest Nagel and James R. Newman, *Gödel's Proof* (New York, 1964); for an extended interpretation of Gödel's theorem see Barkley Rosser, "Extensions of Some Theorems of Gödel and Church" (Sept., 1936), 1 *Journal of Symbolic Logic* 87-91; for a simplified version of Rosser's interpretation see Nagel and Newman, *ibid.*, pp. 91-2, n. 28; for the view that Gödel's theorem does not establish the superiority of natural over artificial intelligence see J.J.C. Smart, *Philosophy and Scientific Realism* (London, 1963), pp. 116-21 and 128-9.
[40] *Supra*, p. 55 n. 29, p. 221.
[41] See Eric Toms, *Being, Negation and Logic* (Oxford, 1962) p. 5.

consequence which affords substantial theoretical justification for the topical approach to problem solving.[42]

In a system which provides computability, "transformation rules" guarantee consistency with those of the formal language we call arithmetic for "elementary algebra has been deliberately designed so that its transformation rules are consistent with arithmetical language."[43] However, according to Gödel's theorem, each wider, important system is faced with system-generated propositions whose affirmation or denial can neither be proved nor disproved.[44]

This theorem affects computer operations as the validity of their results is tested by the notion of "effective procedure."[45] An ideal procedure consists of a system of rules which tells us in precise and unambiguous language what to do from one moment to the next. A computer procedure is effective if it is based on a knowledge of the systematic behaviour rules for the machine. It assumes the equivalence of an understanding of these rules to the knowledge of the thing itself. The distinction between a map of a city and familiarity with the city itself illustrates the assumption. An understanding of the familiar[46] may however rest on intuitions that we are unable to explicate except in metaphors.[47] If so, the program may grossly misrepresent the theory which provides the approach to the solution of a problem. In this case, the computer will misbehave.[48]

The procedure has not only to be effective from a logical point of view, it has to be "naturally" effective, if the procedure is to achieve a congruence between the rules of logic and the facts to which they refer. However, all the requirement of effectiveness achieves is that any process we can describe in terms suitable for a logic machine is an effective procedure, and vice versa.[49] Advocates of automatic fact-finding and decision-making processes suggest a way out of this circle. Their argument is twofold. First, that it is a mistake to assume that a program is an inherently precise and rigid medium of expression. Second, that it is misleading to assert the computer does only what its programmer told it to do as a program is a heuristic search that tries various arrangements and moves.[50] The similarity of these

---

[42] See this text, pp. 12-13 and 27-28.
[43] See Joseph Weizenbaum, *supra*, n. 29, p. 68.
[44] Nagel and Newman, *supra*, p. 57 n. 39 and pp. 45-47, 90-93.
[45] *Ibid.*, pp. 63 and 157.
[46] See *supra*, p. 10.
[47] *Cf.*, *supra*, p. 2.
[48] *Supra*, n. 29, p. 65.
[49] *Ibid.*, p. 63.
[50] Marvin Minsky, "Why Programming is a Good Medium for Expressing Poorly-understood and Sloppily-formulated Ideas," *Design and Planning 2, Computers in Design and Communication*, Martin Krampen and Peter Seitz eds. (New York, 1967), p. 117 at pp. 120 and 121.

explanations with the use of topics in problem solving[51] is however deceptive. There is a critical difference between the topical approach and the arrangements and moves of a programmer. In the former mode the meaning context of the surroundings is harmonized with a meaning of an appearance whose configuration cannot be derived from the properties of its elements. However, when a programmer tries to imitate the solver of a problem in actual decision-making, he finds that his scope is limited to those appearances which can be described by computation. This limitation commits him to systemic procedures however greatly he wishes to emancipate himself from them. In contrast, solution of actual problems is not constrained by the binary model of computerized decision-making.

The requirement that a procedure not only be effective but also that the effectiveness be "natural" is needed in order to determine what a computer can and should be told. If, however, there are things we know but can tell only metaphorically, these are by fiat excluded from the circle of knowable things. To support the argument that fact-finding with and without the insertion of the computer in the decision-making process are equivalent, one would have to grant a monopoly to realist doctrines.[52]

The advocates of artificial intelligence have prepared a further defensive position. This is the denial that Gödel's theorem points to a radical flaw in systemic order. With specific reference to computer operations it is argued that the thesis applies strictly only to perfectly self-consistent logical systems and that in practice these are irrelevant.[53] One has to ask in what relaxed manner the thesis applies to systems which are not perfectly self-consistent. Does it apply at random, and if so, would it render the results of computer operations more trustworthy?

The difficulties which have been outlined snowball in practice. Typically, the programmer does not understand the structural or substantive problems to which the program addresses itself.[54] His primary concern is with the formal validity of his manipulations of symbols according to precise transformation rules. In seeking to reduce complex decision-making processes to hierarchies of binary choices, he

---

[51] See *supra*, pp. 9, 10 and 14.
[52] This reference is to the central thesis of philosophical Realism in its traditional form that universals together with logical and mathematical entities have real existence; for a defense of this thesis see Joseph Lebacqz, *De l'Identique au Multiple* (Louvain and Quebec, 1968). In modern philosophy the term "Realism" refers to the thesis that material objects exist independently of experience. Jurisprudential Realism, in its "devotion to facts, and nothing but facts" (*Dias on Jurisprudence*, 2nd ed. (London, 1964), Ch. 19, p. 370) has an affinity with the modern school of philosophical Realism.
[53] See *supra*, n. 50, p. 118.
[54] *Supra*, n. 29, p. 119.

will modify the routine of the program or enlarge it by the addition of subroutines. He will understand the behaviour of a subroutine without necessarily understanding how it converts the input given to it to the output which is delivered.[55]

Being primarily technologists, programmers tend to treat errors in the output as technical errors and not as errors in understanding.[56] Frustrations result which the programmer tries to overcome by further modifications or the addition of further subroutines but this "invariably causes some of the substructures of the program to collapse" as the modifications or additions will turn the program into "an amorphous collection of processes whose interactions with one another are virtually fortuitous."[57]

So far only the activities of the single programmer have been considered. The margin of error increases with the new practice of using multi-console computers. There, "no one of the programmers will understand it all."[58] Moreover, these programmers are expected to work independently of each other. The reason given for this arrangement is that a program is a heuristic search.[59] In sum, the programmer is exhorted to simulate the behaviour of research scientists engaged in original work. Two characteristics distinguish the former from the latter. Programmers lack the background and the experience of the research scientist. Further, the task consists in converting concrete into abstract meanings in strict obedience to systematically ordered transformation rules. This procedure will obscure the uniqueness which is the hallmark of a discovery.

It is then recommended to use superprogrammers instead of programmers.[60] This demand brings to mind certain reformers of the law whose claims are realizable only if superjudges sit on the bench. It is further argued that the upgrading of the task of the programmer is needed in any case as a program should no longer be considered as an information processing device but as a "court of law" to which issues of interpretation are being submitted. Accordingly the specifications written by programmers are to be considered as rules of evidence for the adjudication of the behaviour of little societies.[61] The first reaction of a lawyer may be that imitation is the sincerest form of flattery. However, only those lacking practical experience in juridical fact finding, in which the problem of the cumulation of circumstantial evidence looms large, will see an affinity between computer operations

---

[55] *Ibid.*, p. 104.
[56] *Ibid.*, p. 243.
[57] *Ibid.*, p. 120.
[58] *Supra*, n. 50, p. 121.
[59] See *supra*, p. 58.
[60] *Supra*, n. 50, p. 121.
[61] *Ibid.*, pp. 119 and 120.

and the legal process. Moreover, this presumed affinity could be used to buttress the claim that scientific matters and especially technology assessments be taken out of the control of the courts and entrusted to the computer. The epithet of "terrified humanists" who "rhapsodize about the obscurity of thought processes"[62] can be borne here with equanimity. In any case, to reply in kind would not answer the purpose of these inquiries.

Two decisions illustrate the matter. In *Diaz v. Gonzales*,[63] Holmes, J., had this to say in regard to the cultural surroundings of a case:

> . . . to one brought up in [a given culture], varying emphasis, tacit assumptions, unwritten practices, a thousand influences gained only from life, may give to the different parts wholly new values that logic and grammar never could have got from the books.

In *Boykowych v. Boykowych*[64] Mr. Justice Rand places the juridical fact-finding task into its proper perspective.

> But what is the 'nature' of the fact in issue? The fact may have physical, religious, moral, ethical, social, legal or other characteristics and implications and its 'nature' in the sense in which acts are weighed and judged by a community cannot escape the influence of most of these senses of the civilized human intelligence by which judgment is made. Our every day judgments are reached after weighing circumstances on the scale of experience but in the presence of these characterizing circumstances.

The shortcomings of computerized fact finding become acute when a single central installation serves a whole range of departments or enterprises. In this way, control is exercised not only over the collection and evaluation of facts but also over the access to the information which had been processed. In some areas governmental evaluations of technological processes amount already to a complete control over assessments.

The tendency towards the proliferation of subroutines by frustrated programmers[65] may be considered as the behaviour of *homo ludens* who grants to the rules of the game the status of — postulated — laws of nature. His close connection with man as the maker of myths has often been pointed out. Characteristic of many cosmologies is their mechanistic structure. It promotes quantifications of the relation between means and ends so that output becomes predictable.[66] In its role of explicator and predictor the machine becomes itself a myth and the operations a ritual which fascinates. It is a myth that celebrates the rationality of the relations between the appearances in the world. The celebration reaches

---

[62] *Ibid.*, pp. 120 and 117.
[63] 261 U.S. 102 (1923), 67 L. Ed. 550, 552.
[64] [1955] S.C.R. 151 at 155.
[65] See nn. 29 and 50.
[66] *Cf., supra*, p. 40.

a new climax in computer operations. By mechanizing the language in which the orders are given the computer is capable of controlling the operations of all the other automata. This is the strength of the "rational actor" model in decision making and the allure of *maximin* and *minimax* computations.[67] It also explains the failure of theoretical objections to induce technology to change its direction. Only lived experience can do this. Even so, the triviality of machine simulations of intelligent behaviour, the insensitivity of the computer to ongoing change, its failure to account for group decision and the dependence of the agent on the machine show themselves already with a poignancy that can no longer be blunted by mere promises that "further research" will find the cure.

We have indicated that the programmer or rather programmers, when modifying programs or adding subroutines, lack understanding of the substantive matters involved and that these interventions are reaching a stage where no one is any longer capable of understanding even the formal aspects of the operation. We have further seen that this decisive defect is expected to be curable by computer simulations of legal procedures. Yet lawyers know only too well that the formal structures of the juridical process are instrumentalities for making decisions on substantive matters. They know that outside of routine matters considerations of form are in fact finding, secondary to trustworthy description. An overview of present trends confirms this. In many branches of the law one discerns a dissatisfaction with taxonomies based on formal criteria. The more systematic they are, thereby conforming to the "rational actor" model, the more vulnerable they show themselves to the impact of change. Of the examples which come to mind are the ongoing reforms of rules of pleading and evidence and the rejection of formal criteria for the determination of a *ratio decidendi*.[68] In these and other fields there is an ongoing search for the appropriate parameters of the fact-finding task. The factors which tip the balance in the particular case cannot be computed and formalized. In each case, the judges know what is required but there are no means of telling it all to the computer. The "rational actor" model in which computability is the link between means and ends is inadequate to this task.[69]

We can now see the origins of the parallel between "knowing" and "telling" in the rhetorical question, "What do judges know that we cannot tell a computer?" It is the claim that the relevant connexions between language and things can be symbolically expressed in logical and mathematical notations and that the axioms and transformation

---

[67] See *supra*, p. 53.
[68] I.e., "The point in a case which determines the judgment," *Black's Law Dictionary*, 4th ed. (St. Paul, Minn., 1951), p. 1429. The use of the metaphor "point" is significant in itself, *cf.*, *supra*, p. 46.
[69] *Cf.*, *supra*, p. 60.

rules of these disciplines provide the means of a faithful description of the appearance of the world. To consider this claim, an excursion into a domain where the problems are perennial was needed. This excursion is not being made voluntarily. It is being imposed upon the law by the magnitude of the claims of computer science. It may be objected that their consideration amounts to a journey into foreign parts, and that the law is not equipped for the journey. However, we have seen that precisely those computer-scientists, who make the most sweeping claims for the merits of their machines, invoke the legal process as model.[70] This gives the law a standing in the matter as only lawyers can know from their lived experience the scope and capabilities of their discipline.

Once we have overcome the initial incredulity that the structural congruence of knowledge with computability is being asserted in earnest, we ask ourselves for explanations. These may be found in the general tendency of behaviour to stretch its reach regardless of the risk of overreaching. Whenever an obstacle is being encountered, means are sought to overcome it, to transcend it. If descriptions are needed to determine facts and the limitations of natural language impede the fact-finding task, alternative means of descriptions are sought. A combination of two techniques offers itself. One is the displacement of natural language by a formal language manipulated according to a system of transformation rules which claims to be self-consistent. The other technique consists in excluding qualitative descriptions. This has an ironic consequence. A "legislative" limitation is substituted for the limitations inherent in descriptions made in natural language. Being "legislative" in character, this limitation generates interpretational problems of its own. The problems reveal the ambiguity and circularity of the notion of a naturally effective procedure. Inherent in this notion is the assertion of the structural congruence of the thing that is being described with its description. However, the argument moves in a circle, as we cannot effectively describe effectiveness. The notion of a computer procedure that is naturally effective rests on beliefs of which "The world has a logical structure" or "God is a mathematician" are examples.

A cosmological thread runs from stoic doctrines to Newton and to Einstein's General Theory of Relativity. The characteristic common to these hypotheses is the effort of describing dynamics of change in terms of mechanics of motion.[71] A passage in Cicero epitomizes the underlying view of the world:

---

[70] The principle of causality in its form of a one-to-one relation provides the basis for this model of rationality. It pre-supposes a primordial simplicity of the structure of the world.

[71] A prime example is Spinoza's attempt to link mathematics and humanities by establishing an ethics *de more geometrico*.

In the firmament, therefore, there is no accident, no chance, no aimless wandering, nothing untrustworthy. On the contrary, all things display perfect order, reliability, purpose, constancy.... Wherefore, that man who holds that the astounding orderliness of the world and the incredible precision of movement of these celestial bodies upon which the support and safety of all things are wholly dependent, are not directed by reason must himself be considered to be utterly devoid of the rational faculty.[72]

In their historical perspective the foregoing inquiries should be viewed not only as criticism of particular manifestations of technology but also as objections to the general direction into which it is being pushed or is thrusting itself by its own momentum. Moreover, these objections cannot be considered in isolation. They involve a reappraisal of the civilizational and cosmological aspects which form the surroundings of a technology. It is perhaps not too far fetched to hear in the protests against the stupefying ubiquity of the computer as decision-maker an echo of the Greek opposition to the megasolutions which had been adopted in the great river basins of the East. This opposition was supported by a searching criticism of the institutions which protected these solutions. Today, however, the surviving evidence of these initiatives and of their failure is being suppressed by the anti-historism of technology. If the law wishes to keep a neutral stance in adjudicating the articulations of sociality,[73] it would have to shed certain accretions that owe more to ideologies than to common sense. Regarding the juridical fact-finding task, the place to start is not the rules of evidence but the rules of procedure. They form the threshold on which the legal process begins and to a large extent determine what can be said about the facts of a case and how to say it.

---

[72] *De natura deorum II*, 56; on the notion of orderliness see *supra*, pp. 14 and 15.
[73] *Cf., supra.* p. 47.

Chapter 5

Procedure and Evidence

ATOMIC FACTS

What can be said and how to say it is indicated by the rules of procedure. They provide the framework for the resolution of the dispute. As contest, the trial provides a spectacle which entertains and in entertaining educates, although the causalities which are involved are obscure. The contest has been described as follows:

> He has two antagonists: The first pushes him from behind . . . The second blocks the road in front of him. He struggles with both. Actually the first supports him in his struggle with the second, for the first wants to push him forward; and in the same way the second supports him in his struggle with the first; for the second of course is trying to force him back. But it is only theoretically so. For it is not only the true protagonists who are there, but he himself as well, and who really knows his intentions? . . . he (may) spring out of the fighting line and . . . on account of his experience of such warfare, . . . judge . . . his struggling antagonists.[1]

The allegory retains verisimilitude even in the most ordinary common law action where, to use the hyperbole of Hewart, C.J., the parties argue over the responsibility for "the collision between two stationary motorcars."[2]

The ancient *clameur de Haro:* "*A l'aide, mon prince, on m'a fait tort*" may be considered a prototype of the procedural claim, and the writ system its subsequent formalization.[3] An action over an executory contract[4] is a world apart from that launched with the *clameur de Haro*. Interests in land have permanence and the type of title of the holder is known publicly, whereas the stipulations of executory contracts differ greatly and the contract comes to an end with its performance. Pleadings are needed here in order to specify the content of the stipulation in issue.

With the reception into the common law of the Mediterranean law

---

[1] Franz Kafka, *Description of a Struggle* (London, 1960), p. 299; throughout his working life, the author was a practising lawyer.
[2] Quoted in H.G. Hanbury, *English Courts of Law*, 4th ed. (London, 1967), p. 118.
[3] In the Channel Islands, this Norman commencement of litigation seems to have survived for certain disputes over land.
[4] *I.e.*, containing obligations to be met in the future.

merchant,[5] an offspring of the *ius gentium*,[6] the monetary obligations of commerce became freely enforceable. This made the older forms of action of debt and *assumpsit* redundant.[7] The organization of the mobility of the claims and obligations in commercial contracts required a conceptual framework. The abstractions which were achieved in this way influenced the rules of pleading. The link between the claim and the pleading which supports it acquired a logical form and the same logic governed the internal structure of the pleading. In these rules we look at a chain of traditions which stretch from the Aristotelian syllogism to its refinement by the Stoics, from the *ius gentium* to the law schools of Northern Italy, whence it reached into the rules of pleading of the common law. The logical strength of the monetary claim in contract was reflected in the two available alternatives of the decision. Two significant exceptions, established in the last century, come to mind. The first is the power of a County Court to allow a defendant to pay his debt in installments fixed by the court. The other is a provision in the German law of obligations that debts are to be discharged equitably and in good faith.[8] It is worth mentioning that this provision became the basis for the initial measures of revaluation of mortgage and other long-term debts after they had lost their value in the inflation following the first World War.

Equity cuts across the certainties of the common law and its procedural rules reflected this contrast. It was the practice in Equity to conclude the Bill — no Writ was required — with a prayer for "such further or other relief as this Honourable Court may deem meet." This prayer infringes on the logical alternatives of granting or refusing orders in accordance with the allegations or denials of common law pleadings. Common law procedure sought to isolate a cause of action from its surroundings, procedure in Equity to harmonize it with them. The jurisdiction of the Lord Chancellor allowed for solutions which mediated between the aims of the parties. This mediating power is apparent in the equitable reliefs, the remedy of the injunction and the tort of nuisance.

The traces of this development have been obscured, first by the Judicature Act 1873 and the corresponding Law Declaratory Acts in force in outlying common law jurisdictions, and later by the reluctance of Equity to increase the classes of suits in which equitable remedies and reliefs were available.[9] In our times certain characteristics of procedure

---

[5] True to the intrinsic character of the common law, the reception was unsystematic.
[6] The rules of law common to all nations.
[7] Old forms of action for the enforcement of formally and informally made contracts, respectively.
[8] Para. 242 of the German Civil Code.
[9] See however Sir Raymond Evershed, M.R., "Equity must Not be Presumed to be Past

in Equity press for recognition in respect of the legislation which issues from the interventionist state. This legislation may have different perspectives from that of the traditional statute law. Typically, the latter directed itself against isolated mischiefs whereas contemporary legislation is more concerned with comprehensive policies conceived to promote or protect a new public interest or interest of the public. This change is of crucial importance in the adjudicative fact-finding task. Notwithstanding the logical stringency which the new legislation may display in its statutory definitions and the code-like arrangement of its provisions, its operating concepts are often more diffused, more value-laden than those of the statute law of former times. This allows for and requires a mediating flexibility in granting remedies. In this respect they have more affinity with Equity than with the common law. This development affected issues of relevance.[10] Instead of being firmly grounded in a familiar legal institution, the relevance of a particular allegation of fact will now be problematic instead of being determinable by straight-line deduction from the norm. For the rules of pleading faithful description has become as important as logical analysis.

The traditional fact-finding task depended on the polarity of true and false. The times are however past when canons of verification or falsification provided full scientific support for this polarity. It had to be abandoned when it was found that the gap between principle and instance is occupied by a series of meta-theses which array themselves in a regress which begins with the theory of a theory and continues accordingly *ad infinitum*.

A related regression is being encountered when the polarity of true and false is mediated by a third value which in the law is indicated by the Scottish verdict of "not proven." A formal three-valued logic can be constructed but it opens the way to four-, five- and so on - valued logics and from there to an infinitely valued one. The complexities of these multi-valued logics would overwhelm the fact-finding task. Significant is here the solution that has been found in scientific explanation and prediction. In a comment on the quantum theory we find the following explanation:

> For, although the final statements (quantum theory) makes concerning the results of sub-atomic experiments are two-valued ("true" or "false", Boolean) in character, the route by which they are obtained clearly involves something more. The particles are treated as waves, and the probability of finding them at particular places depends on the reinforcement or cancellation of mutually interfering trains of waves. In other words, the relative phase of a

---

the Age of Child Bearing" (1953), 1 *Syd. L.R.* 1; *cf., Moate v. Moate*, [1948] 2 All E.R. 486 and *Wirth v. Wirth* (1956), 98 C.L.R. 228 at pp. 237-8.

[10] The distinctions which at times are being made between "material" and "relevant" allegations of fact are not of critical importance and the terms will therefore be treated as synonyms; *cf., Phipson on Evidence*, 10th ed., para. 157.

wave enters into, complicates and enriches the underlying logic of quantum mechanics. The phase drops out in the subsequent calculation of the probability of a given experimental result because it is assumed that it should do so — in other words it is assumed that there can be only one correct evaluation. While this assumption of a two-valued "true" or "false" logic had had great utility as an approximation in existing physics, the theory should allow incomplete deductions of a three-value type ("true," "false" and "partly true") to be made. This will, and this is essentially the point of "triality," be necessary if we are to succeed in reconciling quantum theory with cosmology, and making itself consistent.[11]

The choices between hypotheses according to the verification or falsification principle are burdened by the problem of finding a logical form for the criterion of simplicity. The elucidations which so far have been made do not encourage an expectation that formal logic will lead to a solution of this problem.[12]

Before noting recent changes in the rules governing a fact-finding task, certain underlying presuppositions need to be considered. A typical norm contains a description in general terms of that which "ought to or may or must not be or be done."[13] Hence, rules of pleading sought to establish the general conditions in which the isomorphy of a pleading with the fact content of a norm can be shown. The main feature of the traditional rules of pleading was their systematic-deductive character. Its justification was the supposition that the domain of facts had the same character. A notable description of this domain is given in the *Tractatus*.[14] This work sought to determine the limitations which formal logic encounters in constructing a mirror that reflects the structure of the world. The work culminates in a critique of the axiomatics which a logical description of facts requires. It appeared at a stage in physics when the certainties of Rutherford were giving way to the uncertainties of Heisenberg. In this crisis, influential circles seized upon the *Tractatus* and in particular its truth tables (4.27-4.431) as the means of converting metaphysics into formal logic. The ultimate aim was to turn philosophy into a hand maiden of the "exact" sciences.

So profoundly was the main thrust of the *Tractatus* misunderstood or ignored that during his lifetime Wittgenstein withheld his further

---

[11] McGoodall, "The Changing Structure of Science" (1963), 20 *New Scientist* 254 at p. 255; on the motive in upholding the requirement of consistency see Nicholas Rescher, *The Primacy of Practice* (Oxford, 1973), Ch. V, esp. p. 103; see also Roy L. Stone-de Montpensier, "Logic and Law: The Precedence of Precedents" (1967) *Minn. L.R.* 655 at pp. 658, 662, 664 and 668.

[12] For the present state of these investigations see Elliott Sober, *Simplicity* (Oxford, 1975), pp. 33, 60-68, 171 ss.

[13] Georg Henrik von Wright, *Norm and Action* (London, 1963), p. 71.

[14] Wittgenstein, *Tractatus Logico-Philosophicus* (London, 1922), in the following pages figures in brackets indicate the numbers of the propositions in the *Tractatus*; the original German text is printed on facing pages.

writings from publication. However, one cannot be certain whether these misinterpretations or the author's subsequent change of position on semantic problems were responsible for this decision.

There are structural similarities between misinterpretation of the *Tractatus* and the popular conception of Platonism. They show the strength of the preference of the simple to the complex in the search for the link between belief and reason. Plato's fame rested on his theory of Forms in which they were elevated to a "sphere above the heavens."[15]

The forms or ideas were eternal and the temporal things their copies. Their ontological dependence prevented them from participating fully in the forms, resulting in a separation of their spheres. Plato then saw that this separation led to a cosmology in which a god could as little avail himself of the ideas in order to comprehend the sphere of things as man, an exile in this sphere, could comprehend the ideas. In *Parmenides* Plato reconstructed his theory of the two spheres by stipulating a continuous, progressive descent and ascent between them, in which the ideas intertwine and participate not only in each other but also in the things. In this way he expected to demonstrate the primordial coincidence of "being" and "reason". This attempt to give a logical form to this unity failed when on imagining the idea of an idea an infinite regress was encountered. On discovering this, Plato blamed his method but clung to his original transcendental conception.[16] History refused to acknowledge the revision of the earlier thesis of the separation of the spheres. In the western world, important views subscribed to the radical dualism which Plato had proclaimed only to reject it later. Historically the concatenation extends from the construct of a "sphere above the heavens" to a rationality in which the "cosmic mind" stipulated by Neo-Platonism became the *intellectus divinus* of mediaeval metaphysicists. Kant's "transcendental subject" is a further step in this direction. In modern times it became the bearer of theoretical knowledge whose truth science was ready to confirm.

Radical dualism is deeply embedded in legal theories of the West. Each adjudicative decision was expected not only to resolve disputes but also to sit in judgment on itself in order to vindicate transcending values. It is the glory as well as the burden of the Platonic heritage in the law, a burden that under the impact of sweeping change is becoming increasingly heavy to bear.

These perspectives form a background for the theory of atomic facts which underlies the traditional rules of pleadings.

According to the *Tractatus* "the world divides into facts" (1.2). The verb "divide" is used absolutely in this statement in which "fact" is a

---

[15] *I.e.*, dwelling in the "place above the heavens" see *Phaedrus,* 247 C; *cf., Republic* Bk. VII, 520 D.

[16] *Parmenides,* 133A, 140E, 158B and 160A.

synonym for that which "is the case" (2). The verb is followed by a prepositional clause which points to the result of the division. Early lessons in arithmetics have made this usage familiar. In this way, the proposition asserts that the experience of the divisibility of the world into singularities, the relation between a whole and its parts, between a process and its events, is confirmed by the regularities of logical operations. The use of the verb "divide" implies further that the distinctions we make between a whole and its parts and between one part and another are similar in kind to the absolute distinction which obtains between one number and any other. The unexpected context in which the verb "divide" here appears tends to lean its meaning towards that of the expression "consists."

In comparing the English and German versions of this proposition[17] we find that the latter does not use the conventional German equivalent of "divide," i.e., *teilen* of its compounds. Instead, we read the expression *zerfaellt*. The stem of this verb is the same in both languages, as seen in "fall" and "fallen" respectively, and so is their meaning of a descent or lowering. The German prefix *zer* signifies disintegration or destruction. The compound verb-form which is here being used describes the collapse or doom of a structure. This meaning is strengthened by a further circumstance. The Latin equivalent of the verb "fall" is *cadere* from which the English noun "case" is derived. Originally it denoted a thing that "befalls."[18] In German "case" means "Fall" so that the German noun has retained its original meaning of descent which the expression "case" no longer has. In particular, the biblical fall is no longer hinted at by the expression "case" but this meaning is retained by the German counterpart "Fall." The more one looks at the verb *zerfaellt* in the original version of proposition 1.2, the stronger becomes the whiff of corruption emanating from it.[19]

In any case, the German verb indicates change and has a concrete character, while the English has predominantly an abstract meaning which invokes the immunity to change of the rules of algebra.

A Faustian ambition to create a language that, thanks to its logical structure, is free of the latencies, ambiguities and disorders of natural language is then a means of escaping from the corruption of this world. Computer language is a reflection of the language spoken in "the place above the heavens" and so deserving the awe in which it is being held. The search for a purely logical language is sustained not only by hybris[20]

---

[17] *Supra*, n. 14, pp. 6 and 7.
[18] *S.O.E.D.*, 3rd ed., p. 290; see also *supra* n. 14, p. 68, which in the index shows this German equivalent of "case."
[19] It is conceded that the translators were facing a difficult task. The synoptic presentation of original and translation absolves them however of the reproach to mislead.
[20] This Greek term is widely understood to denote "overweening pride"; for a critique of

but also by deep feelings of dissatisfaction. Feelings of this kind animate the shifts in orientation from the singular person towards the group and vice versa.[21]

The division of the world into facts is the premise for the conclusion that "each item can be the case or not the case while everything else remains the same" (1.21). It will be noted that descriptions given in the earlier part of this inquiry[22] are at odds with this critically important proposition. They showed the inability of the operations of formal logic to cope with the dynamics of change except by presenting tautologics. The propositions of the *Tractatus* demonstrate this at the level of formal logic itself. "What is the case — a fact — is the existence of a state of affairs" (2) and "A state of affairs (a state of things) is a combination of objects (things)" (2.01). Hence, if there is a change in the surroundings of a thing concomitant with its own change, then both the thing and the part of the surroundings involved form one state of affairs, and if there is no change in the surroundings of a fact upon a change of the fact itself, then the fact and its surroundings form separate states of affairs. In this way the parameter, determined by the range of the change, will always be correct. The notion of entity is formed quantitatively by the parameter. On this basis it becomes possible to claim "Every statement about complexes can be resolved into a statement about their constituents and into the propositions that describe the complexes completely (*sic*)" (2.0201).

By means of logico-mathematical operations but not otherwise can one represent to oneself what it would be like for the world to change in some respect and in no other. In these operations identity is determined by the possibilities, which definitions and analysis allow, for changes in the rate and range of change. It is therefore not surprising that values are not included in the description of the world given by the *Tractatus*. They do not belong in the world, they are "transcendental" and cannot be described (6.4-6.422).

This passage has been exploited by the defenders of the value ascesis which technology practises. Nowhere, except in aesthetics, is the result of a logical operation more precarious than in the fact-finding task of the law. There, much of the evidence is circumstantial, and proof is being established not only by an analysis of the adduced evidence but also and decisively so by a process of cumulation. Circumstantial proof is made by weaving threads of evidence which by themselves are weak into a strand whose breaking strength is not quantifiable. There is more to the process of cumulation than quantification and this "more" consists in

---

this conception see Walter Kaufmann, *Tragedy and Philosophy* (New York, 1969), s. 15, pp. 68 ss.
[21] *Supra,* p. 40.
[22] *Supra,* pp. 1, 5, 13, 17, and 24.

the discovery of the configuration of the state of affairs under scrutiny. The final step in the process of cumulation is the value judgment on the facts. If the reasons for this judgment cannot be shown by means of the transformation rules of formal logic, it is however more likely to be the fault of logic than that of the value judgment. Bearing in mind the unsolvable logical paradoxes[23] and the ambushes of systematization which formal logic encounters, there is no justification for these rules to proclaim themselves as the exclusive arbiters of rationality. In particular, formal logic is not justified to deprecate the topical approach[24] to the problem of cumulating circumstantial evidence. Ultimately, what is at stake here is not the right but the best decision in the concrete case.

Using the terms of the *Tractatus*, the allegations of fact in a Statement of Claim are propositions about states of affairs. A state of affairs is a combination of things and the minimum requirement for its description is a sentence consisting of a subject and one attribute joined by the copula as in the proposition "The cat is on the mat" which according to proposition 1.21 can be the case or not be the case while everything else remains the same. Further, every statement about a complex can be resolved into a statement about its constituents. In the result, the world is "divided" into discrete or atomic facts to which the structure of their description can correspond with the help of symbols. Facts and descriptions move in the same "logical space" (1.13 and 2.0201). This enables us to make a logical picture of the world (3). It should be noted that the observer is treated here as just another atomic fact or complex of atomic facts.

However, logic moves in tautologies (6.126-6.1263) and the propositions made in a logical language are formulae which indicate the transformations within the language.[25] Yet, formal logic, this is to say a systematization, is claimed by the *Tractatus* to mirror the world (4.121, 5.511 and 6.13). If so, fact finding is a juggling with mirrors which have the diffractionary power to discern atomic facts. An atomic fact is then at midpoint of the oscillation of logic between the vacuity of its tautologies (*cf.*, 4.462) and the scandal of its paradoxes. The fact content of a norm, which shows an ideal situation, is reflected at this midpoint.

---

[23] The paradox of the sophist's fee, payable only after the student wins his first lawsuit, is one of the many early examples of a self-reflective paradox. In his first suit the student seeks a declaration that he is not obligated to pay the fee. If the student loses, he need not pay qua contract and if he wins, qua judgment; the best known of these paradoxes is that of the Cretan who states that all Cretans are liars; it reduces itself to the undecidable question whether the statement "I am lying" is true or false; it is here noteworthy that the reasoning involved in Gödel's theorem is modeled on the self-reflective "Richard Paradox;" for its description and critique see Nagel and Newman, *supra*, p. 57 n. 39, pp. 60-3 and 90 n. 27.

[24] *Supra*, pp. 11-13 and 27-28.

[25] *Cf., supra*, pp. 62-63.

From the conventional scientific point of view this construction or rather flight of imagination makes the assimilation of a legal norm to the "laws of nature" possible. To comply with the transformation rules of formal logic, change has to be reduced to the differential calculus or ignored altogether. The logically inaccessible dynamics of change are beyond the ambit of these rules. This exclusion is required as in logic there are no surprises (2.012 and 6.1251).

PLEADINGS

There are strong affinities between the theory of atomic facts presented in the *Tractatus* and the structure of the traditional rules of pleading.[26] This correspondence can be seen more clearly in the rules governing denials than in those governing allegations of fact. According to the *Tractatus*, both "the existence and non-existence of states of affairs is a reality" (2.06). On terming an existing state of affairs a positive and its non-existence a negative fact, a positive proposition presupposes the existence of the negative proposition and vice versa (5.5151). One of the several ways of attempting to determine the meaning of negation as such is to stipulate for it the following requirements: a propositional character so that there shall be one and only one negation of a given proposition; reciprocality, so that if one proposition negates the other, the latter negates the former; mutual exclusiveness; and joint exhaustion, so that it must be the case that one or the other must be true.[27] The insistence on the requirement of joint exhaustion is questionable as an alternative logic may be formulated which ignores the laws of the excluded middle. This alternative can be justified on the ground that the law of the excluded middle is not derivable from the other axioms of logic.[28] In this alternative logic, the double negation has to be weaker than the affirmation[29] and the triple negation the equivalent of the simple negation.[30]

There is the initial difficulty in the denial of x being y that it may leave it open whether the negation refers to y only or to the entire proposition. Further, a negative proposition may point to an indefinite range of affirmations. Suppose the allegation is that p is more than x feet long. The opposite claim is that p is less than x feet long. The

---

[26] Regarding the problems created by the use of the term "fact" in rules of pleading W.W. Cook, "Facts and Statements of Fact" (1937), 4 *Chicago L.R.* 233 at p. 245 concludes that solutions to the problem of pleading nothing but facts can be found "on the basis of convenience."

[27] See p. 68 n. 13, p. 138.

[28] See Robert Feys, "Logik", in *Die Philosophie des XX. Jahrhunderts*, Fritz Heinemann ed. (Stuttgart, 1963), p. 320.

[29] In classical Greek and in Chaucer the double negation may mean a strong negation.

[30] See *supra*, n. 28.

proposition contained in this denial is inconsistent with that contained in the allegation. However, although inconsistent, the proposition leaves it open that p is x feet long. This proposition contradicts and is inconsistent with both of the other two propositions mentioned.

Suppose, however, that the negation takes the form "p is not over x feet long." This general form of denial excludes all third positions; there is no way of making a statement that is inconsistent with both the allegation and the denial. Here, allegation and denial are "contradictories;" in the former example there are only "contraries."[31] The distinction between contraries and contradictories renders good service where an allegation has a quantitative character, this is to say, the magnitude of the predicate can be determined by measurement. This is so because the numbers which the measurement yields have a discrete character with clearly discernible boundaries. It is different with qualitative predicates as values are diffused and permeate a whole.[32]

According to the *Tractatus* a proposition, whether it is positive or negative, is a description of a state of affairs which construct the world with the help of a logical scaffolding (4.023). A universe of discourse of this kind is plagued by a logical Malthusianism. Populated by a multitude of possible positive propositions, it may establish for each of them an indefinite host of negative propositions. We can be thankful to the judges who have refused to apply the ban on evasive pleading *more logico,* preferring to rely on their experience of the world and its affairs to interpret denials within the context in which they were made and other surrounding circumstances. These considerations throw light also on the process of decision making in general and the standards of rationality that should be applied to them. It is now widely recognized that subsumptive reasoning is insufficient to support and explain the decision and that, typically, decisions other than those routinely made are arrived at with the help of analogy for which a "paralogical" status is being claimed.[33] While a logical calculus may be established for the process of subsumption, this cannot be done for the analogy except for trite or artificially constructed situations.[34] The status of denials is a touchstone on which the applicability of rules of formal logic to the interpretation of pleadings can be tested.

Turning to the history of the rules, we find that before the Judicature Acts a general traverse was sufficient. However, in the absence of

---

[31] *See* P.F. Strawson, *Introduction to Logical Theory* (London, 1963), p. 16.
[32] *Supra,* p. 13.
[33] See Roy L. Stone-de Montpensier, *supra,* p. 68 n. 11.
[34] For the assumptions necessary to obtain a calculus of elementary analogical inferences see Mary Hesse, "On Defining Analogy" (1959/60), 60 *Proceedings of Aristotelian Society* 79 and "Analogy and Confirmation Theory" (1964), 31 *Philosophy of Science* 319, especially pp. 321 and 327.

examinations for discovery and in view of the restrictions which logic imposed on the equitable procedure of interrogatories, only time-consuming interlocutory proceedings could elicit the salient relevances ahead of the trial. The Judicature Acts expected to find a remedy in the specific traverse. Logic alone was exempt from the prescription of the specific traverse. A matter whose denial could be established by "necessary implication"[35] was to be treated as if it had been specifically denied. This proviso left it open whether the reference was to formal or to material implication. The use of formal implication presupposes that the allegation, taken to be denied by the fiction which the proviso introduced, is couched in a language that satisfies the requirements of formal logic. This interpretation of the proviso was liable to lead to disputations on problems of formal logic for which a hearing before a Master or Judge in Chambers hardly provided the most suitable forum. Hence, the words "by necessary implication" should be interpreted to mean a material implication. However, this type of reasoning "is not adequate for all the practical inferences of ordinary experience."[36] The distrust of pleaders in the fiction of the equivalence of necessary implication and of specific denial led to the practice of drawing the defence as an inverted mirror image of the Statement of Claim. The abolition of this exercise in futility did not await the comprehensive reform of the B.C. Supreme Court Rules in 1976, which *inter alia* restored the general traverse permissible before the Judicature Acts. Already in 1970 a special amendment was introduced which deleted the words "by necessary implication"[37] thus removing the explicit appeal to the rules of logic in matters of pleading.

---

[35] B.C.S.C. Rules 1961 0.19 r. 13; a comparison of relevant rules will be found on the following page.
[36] See Harold Newton Lee, *Symbolic Logic* (New York, 1961), p. 331.
[37] B.C. *Gazette,* Reg. 91/70.

British Columbia Supreme Court Rules

Order XIX	1961	Rule	1976-
r. 4	Every pleading shall contain, and contain only, a statement in a summary form of the material facts . . . but not the evidence by which they are to be proved.	19(1)	A pleading shall be as brief as the nature of the case will permit and shall contain a statement in summary form of the material facts on which the party relies but not the evidence by which the facts are to be proved.
r. 13	Every allegation of fact in any pleading, not being a petition or notice of motion, if not denied specifically or by necessary implication . . . shall be taken to be admitted . . . . provided that a specific denial may be made of any or all of the allegations	(19)	An allegation of fact in a pleading if not denied or stated to be not admitted . . . shall be taken to be admitted . . . .
		(20)	It is not necessary in a pleading to deny specifically each allegation . . . but a general denial is sufficient with respect to those allegations which are not admitted.
	Phillips v. Ford Motor Co., [1971] 2.O.R. 637 (C.A.) held that in an action, there is no judicial power to order the taking of evidence in respect of any particular fact as this practice would endanger the impartiality of the Court.	28(1)	Where a person, not a party to an action, may have material evidence relating to a matter in question in the action, the Court may order that he be examined . . . .
	see *Beevis v. Dawson*, [1957] 1 Q.B. 195, 216 (C.A.); *Jerome v. Anderson* (1964), 44 D.L.R. 516, 528 (Can. S.C.) on the ban against splitting the case.	40(7)	Where a party omits or fails to prove some fact material to the case, the court may proceed with the trial, subject to that fact being afterwards proved as the Court shall direct . . . .

Federal Court Rules

Rule	Can. Gaz. II, SOR/71-68
408(1)	Every pleading must contain a precise statement of the material facts on which the party pleading relies.
413(2)	Where a party who has pleaded to a pleading . . . has failed to plead to an allegation of fact in that pleading . . . , it shall be assumed that his failure to do so was the result of an oversight and his silence shall not . . . be interpreted as an admission of the truth of that fact.
479(1)	. . . the Court may, before the trial of an action, order that evidence of any particular fact shall be given at the trial in such manner as may be specified by the order.
469(2)	Any time before judgment, the presiding judge may draw the attention of the parties to any gap in the proceedings and permit them to fill it.

EVIDENCE

Reforms of procedural law press for corresponding changes in the rules of evidence. The most important of these concerns expert evidence.[38]

The relevance of the facts to which a scientific expert testifies depends on the scientific explanation which underlies his opinion. As causality is still "the most prominent of all modes of scientific explanation,"[39] we revert once more to the principle which holds that every event has a cause. Traditionally, behind an allegation of fact in a Statement of Claim lies a chain of reasoning which moves from the allegation "S" is "P" to "the P-being S," then from the abstraction "P-being" to "being" as the horizon of the events and from there to the idea in its normative form. In this way the copula "is" stands for the logical subsumption of the object under the concept. The weakness in this chain of reasoning is the causal connexion, an issue which typically cannot be avoided. In Newtonian mechanics which founded a dominant cosmology, causality is a one-to-one relation where the cause is the condition of the effect. Accordingly, the causal judgment should reflect this relation by stating a reciprocal implication of cause and effect. In this formulation of causality however, there is no possibility of distinguishing the one from the other, this is to say there is no distinction between the direction of time in regard to the future and past.

Moreover the developments in microphysics, especially regarding the stochastic processes of radio-active decay, led to theories of the structure of matter which do not ascribe any "causes" to the events under study. These theories point to the probable falsity of the principle of causality. This is not to say that scientific theory excludes from its explanation of an event the operation of a law or laws of nature, it asserts only that an explanation made in probabilistic terms is probably preferable to an explanation made in universalistic, causal terms. With the downgrading of the principle of causality the deductive form of scientific explanation has lost much of its authority. In this type of explanation "the relevant species of evidence furnishes a complete basis for the propositions it supports." Deductive systems of this kind can afford to be completely forward-looking, in that it "is never appropriate to employ a proposition newly arrived at to give additional bolstering and support to one attained at some previous junction." The reverse is true for other evidential systems where "the system of reasoning [may] take the form of a cluster of interlocking propositions lending mutual

---

[38] See Canada Law Reform Commission Study Paper No. 7 on Expert Evidence of July 1973, pp. 23ss and *id.*, *Report on Evidence*, Information Canada, 1975, Catalogue No. J31-15/1975, pp. 40-42 and 97-99; this Report contains the Law Reform Commission draft of an Evidence Code.

[39] See Nicholas Rescher, *Scientific Explanations* (New York, 1970), pp. 121ss.

strength and support to another."[40] It should be a source of satisfaction to the law, an "inexact" science, that physics is now trying to emulate fact-finding procedures which realize the notion of cumulation in assessing indirect, circumstantial evidence.[41]

Further, the selection of relevant facts for a scientific opinion cannot be better than the theory on which it relies. As in modern science a theory has a probabilistic structure, a scientific opinion will be in the form "On the basis of theory P I conclude that S is a fact." We should here not be misled into assuming that the expert is testifying to the truth of S. Not only P but S also has a probabilistic structure. The comparison of the degree of probability of S relative to that of P comes then to the foreground as S cannot have a higher degree of probability than P. On the contrary, in order to find S acceptable as a fact, P should have a higher degree of probability than S in order to serve as explanation.

The foregoing considerations suggest that an explanation for an event which a scientific expert offers in support of his opinion should be given the closest scrutiny and that divergent opinions not be dismissed lightly. In this regard a power of the court to appoint *suo motu*[42] an expert to give his opinion is of crucial importance. This is not to ignore the practical difficulties which may result from the exercise of a judicial power which for so long had been considered obsolete. There is first the question of availability. The proliferation of branches within the established departments of science bear heavily on the task of selection as each branch, to justify its *raison d'être*, tends to be more concerned with the distinctions which sets it apart from adjoining branches than with efforts at integration.[43] On the other hand, the *Phillips* case[44] suggests that in many cases there is an urgent need for a court-appointed expert. In this case a consumer sued a manufacturer. It is noteworthy that the expert witnesses called by the defence held appointments at senior institutions but not the single expert witness called by the plaintiff. There is further the question whether the court-appointed expert should be subject to examination by each party[45] or to cross-examination only as recommended in the Report on the Law of Evidence of the Ontario Law Reform Commission of March 1976. A further question is whether the court-appointed expert can be called upon to express an opinion on the opinions given by the experts called by the parties. A ban on this type of evidence may be difficult to enforce. If

---

[40] For this and the last two previous quotations see *ibid.*, p. 94.
[41] See *supra*, p. 72.
[42] *I.e.*, by a decision made by the adjudicator on his own initiative without an application for it by one of the parties.
[43] *Cf., supra*, pp. 23-24.
[44] *Phillips v. Ford Motor Co.*, [1971] 2 O.R. 637 at 657, 660-2 (C.A.).
[45] *Supra*, p. 77 n. 38, Draft Evidence Code, s. 73(3).

this form of evidence is permitted, the trial judge will have to keep matters firmly in hand in order to prevent the fact-finding task from degenerating into academic disputation. The court will be aided here by the requirement to submit written pre-trial reports[46] on the prospective scientific evidence.

The factual part of the legal process culminates in the argument on the facts. This argument is the bridge from fact-finding to the legal aspects of the decision. The introduction of a court-appointed expert marks a profound change. His opinion and explanation are not part of the case of either party. Each will have to assimilate or reject his evidence and typically neither the assimilation nor the rejection by the party will be complete.

In former times the fact content of a norm often concerned itself only with situations whose consequences were taken for granted. Accordingly, the argument of the plaintiff on the evidence concerned a history of events and a history only. In contrast, modern legislation has a pronounced forward-looking character, concerning itself more with the realization of a policy than the mere suppression of old, specific mischiefs which had become too grave to be any longer ignored by the legislator. For the policy of this type of modern legislation, the predictive or conjectural aspects of expert testimony come to the fore. The hypostatized natural laws provide here less evidential support than they have for the explanation of past events. Again, formerly, there was little need for the defendant to propound a different version; it was often sufficient to show that the evidence failed to support the pleadings of the plaintiff. The defendant had only to show the lack of evidence for a single relevant element of the narrative in order to destroy the case for the plaintiff. This was easiest done where the plaintiff sought to establish a causal relation between the parts of his allegations.

Formerly a probability assessment addressed itself to atomic facts or their complexes.[47] The assessment represented the approximation to the truth or falsity of the fact which human fallibility will permit. With the downgrading or downfall of the principle of causality any proposition of fact may become problematic and the probability assessment a solution which is inherently provisional. Moreover, the ongoing fragmentation of scientific disciplines into sub-branches which close themselves off against each other in order to define themselves better creates problems of their own in the reception of scientific evidence.[48] Specialization encourages dissension. The deductive method will here be of little avail when a choice between conflicting opinions is to be made.

---

[46] See *supra*, p. 77, n. 38, Study Paper No. 7, pp. 34-36.
[47] See *supra*, pp. 69ss.
[48] See *supra*, p. 24.

In a probabilistic universe however different probability assessments may become compatible if they are placed at different levels, each level defining itself only by its relation to the others.

TRYING THE CASE

The grounds on which the Ontario Court of Appeal held in the *Phillips* case[49] that an expert witness should not be appointed by the trial judge, were a concern with the impartiality of the court. Behind these reasons stands the conception that the overall attitude of the trial judge should be one of receptivity. He listens to the evidence which the parties adduce and to the speeches they make and restricts himself otherwise to the general supervision of the course of the trial. It is this passivity which makes it possible for lawyers in many states of the United States of America to consider it a matter of course to say that they, and not the judge, are trying the case. In this view, the performance of the parties are competing causes and the decision the effect of the cause which shows itself to be the more efficient. In order to gauge predictive effectiveness attempts have been made to represent diagrammatically the causal connections within the judicial decision-making process, especially at the collegiate, appellate level.[50] Prediction is made there by means of causal analysis. The overall validity of the reductionist principle of causality and its applicability in a field of psychology is taken for granted.

The diagrams which show the results of this type of research were designed to establish not only sequential causalities but also the dynamic aspects of decision-making. This enterprise is reminiscent of the claim that computer programmers can work heuristically.[51] In both cases there is an attempt to combine the topical approach with a logico-systematic method. However, the reductionist tendency and value-ascesis of the method is incompatible with the perspectives which are opened up in the topical approach. In the result, the decision-maker becomes so entangled in reconciling these two opposing tendencies that a vacuum is liable to occur at the centre of the fact-finding task. The allegory which has been quoted earlier[52] shows that ultimately the judge ceases to be the object of the struggle between the antagonists. At the moment of the decision, he emancipates himself from them. The decision of the Ontario Court of Appeal in the Phillips case sought to

---

[49] See *Phillips v. Ford Motor Co., supra*, n. 44.
[50] See Glendon Schubert, "Two Causal Models of the High Court of Australia," *Comparative Judicial Behaviour*, Glendon Schubert and David J. Danelski, eds. (Toronto, 1969), pp. 365, 343, and 352-3, and Edward J. Weissman, "Mathematical Theory and Dynamic Models," *id.*, pp. 367, 374-5, 384.
[51] See *supra*, p. 60.
[52] See *supra*, p. 65.

protect the impartiality of the judge. But where could it be less threatened than in matters which can be elucidated only by special expertise on which the judge is unlikely to hold firm pre-existing convictions? The danger that the judge forms a special link with the expert whom he appointed is a possibility rather than a probability competing with the relevant probabilities confirmed or disclosed by his opinion. The independence of the adjudicator in the conduct of the fact-finding task is not realized if he is denied the discretion to supplement a systematic approach to fact-finding problems with the topical approach.

As scientific opinion is becoming more uncertain of itself and dependent on the technological systematizations and standardizations of its measuring instruments, the obfuscation of issues becomes a common ploy in disputes involving the evidence of scientific experts. In this situation neither the possibility of shifting the burden of proof according to the degree of plausibility of a particular item of evidence nor the right to lead rebuttal evidence is sufficient for the clarification of a disputed scientific issue.

If the aim of the argument on the facts is to convince by plausibility, the present monologous form of counsel's speech is no longer acceptable. As long as it was believed that scientific theory established scientific truths, a monologue of deductive reasoning could perhaps be accepted as presenting true conclusions. We deliberately used here the qualification "perhaps" as the conclusion that fact P is true because of theory S becomes acceptable only if one turns a blind eye to the inherent defects of the rules of formal logic as they manifest themselves in the logical paradoxes and the inability to hypostatize the operation of material implication. Once the plausibility of a fact is considered against the horizon of probability, the monologue becomes a dangerous weapon as it permits the speaker to weave into his argument fallacies which become effective if the attempt of introducing them is not being promptly checked. In practice this means that the submission on the evidence made by one side should whenever advisable be interrupted by the trial judge or with his permission by the other side in order to clarify the direction of the argument, its precise reference to an alleged fact or to matters of relevance and interpretation. This means a change of the argument on the facts from two monologues, or three if one is adding the reply, to a dialogue or more precisely a trilogy as each statement is addressed not only to the court but also to the opponent either to correct him on a certain point or, at the least, to ensure that the implications of one's own argument on a given point are at all times fully before the court.

These considerations suggest changes also in the manner in which the testimony itself is given. In the classical model the examination of an ordinary witness proceeded by single answers to single questions. This procedure is based on the theory of atomic facts which made it comparatively easy to decide whether the question was relevant and the answer responsive to it. Once it is being recognized that an ordinary witness testifies to a personal experience in the comprehensive meaning of the term, it will be seen that there are distinct advantages in allowing the witness to render the account of his experience as continuously as, according to his testimony, he had lived his singular experience. The risk of having to listen to well-prepared but perjured testimony is being reduced by the increased documentation of most of the transactions which are in dispute. On the other hand, it has become established practice to permit the expert witness to testify without interruptions during his examination-in-chief. What is being suggested here is the reversal of the current practice in which the expert is permitted to give a continuous account and the layman is prevented from doing so. We suggest, further, that the same give and take which should obtain in the argument on the facts between counsel should also be practised in expert testimony. In testimony of more than ordinary significance, the court-appointed expert should participate *seriatim*, the trial judge intervening here only to ensure that he himself has grasped well the scientific theory or fact which is at issue and to see to it that expert testimony does not degenerate into academic disputation, where unfortunately the use of fallacious arguments is not a rare occurrence.

It is one thing to exhort the judge not to permit the degeneration of the fact-finding task into academic disputation, it is another to find the means of realizing this aim. In any controversial matter a balance has to be struck between the willingness to give the parties a full hearing and the need to keep the hearing in manageable proportions. Two aids are available to achieve this: the notions of a shift in the burden of proof, and the possibility of discovering any fallacies which may have been introduced in the interpretation of facts.

The question of burden of proof has been condensed into the maxim, "He who asserts must prove," which provides a starting point for the answer. Factual sequences extend in concatenations in which each complex and linkage awaits proof. The notion of a *prima facie* case and of the presumptions which establish it has been developed from the presumptions of daily life. Here, a shift in the burden of proof means that "In all but the simplest cases ... the burden of the issues is divided, each party having one or more cast upon him."[53] Shifting the burden of proof according to fair presumptions works well enough in cases in which the surrounding facts are familiar. It is different in cases where the evidence of scientific experts is decisive. There, the strange is at issue and it can be rendered familiar only by explanation. Familiarity with the ways of the world is replaced by hypotheses and taxonomies of a

---

[53] *Supra*, p. 67, n. 10, para. 94.

scientific discipline. Typically, these supports of expert opinion are in a process of constant revision. This provides ample opportunity for conflicts of opinion. These conflicts are the rule rather than the exception as experts "are proverbially though perhaps unwittingly, biased in favour of the side which calls them."[54] The value of an expert opinion may be gauged by the explanation which is supplied, and it is for this reason that s. 68 of the Draft Evidence Code permits the examination of a witness with respect to the facts upon which he is relying before giving evidence in the form of an opinion or inference. In expert evidence the relevance of these facts is determined by the scientific theory to which the expert subscribes, and in many cases the conflict of opinion between two experts will depend on the interpretation of several scientific theories or the conflict between them.

A controversy over a matter involving scientific theory can be fruitful only if the two contestants are matched not only in learning but also in adroitness of argument. This will often not be the case, and on this point alone, the court-appointed expert can be of better service than an assessor as the former gives his opinion by examination. Even so, the fallacy in an argument by which a contestant seeks to improve a poor thesis is often not easily detectable. In one of his essays[55] Schopenhauer offers good counsel on detecting fallacies which are frequently encountered in argument.

One of these is to give the proposition of the adversary a broader interpretation than a strict or even a conventional one would permit. One attacks then this enlargement and by refuting it throws suspicion on the original proposition. A similar method is being employed when the consequences of a measure are in dispute. Here one adds a related premise and by combining it with the original one demonstrates a conclusion which defeats the adversary. If one is skilful enough, one may push the proponent entirely away from his original proposition by introducing first a closely related and then, in a series of steps, more remote subjects until the proponent is faced only with this diversion. Unless detected at an early stage, it will lead to the loss of the argument of the proponent.

In submissions on the law of the case, sound legal training makes it comparatively easy to keep the introduction of these fallacies under control. Here, the precedent is capable of performing well as it is an appeal to an authority which is respected. It is different in the fact-finding stage where strictly speaking a finding is typically an inference. Evidence on scientific matters is especially vulnerable.

---

[54] *Ibid.*, para. 1286.
[55] Arthur Schopenhauer, "The Art of Controversy" in *Essays From the Parerga and Paralepomena* (London, 1951), p. 22.

There, minute but significant shifts in argument may be detectable only by those who are learned in the particular discipline to which the subject matter belongs. A fallacy has good prospects of success where several scientific disciplines concern themselves with the same issue of fact so that terminological differences can be fully exploited.[56]

As a fallacy can be described formally and its form is a good aid in detecting it, it would be desirable to acquaint lawyers with the various forms which fallacies can take. Regarding arguments on the facts involving different scientific theories[57] continued legal education could make an important contribution by arranging moot courts in which contradictory expert evidence on presumed theories and assumed facts is being presented.

METAPHYSICS OF FACTS

At the beginning of these inquiries we described the conditions that make experience possible, and the manner in which it gives meanings to behaviour. On this basis we contrasted system building and the topical approach to the solution of a problem. We saw the computer pressing for the maximization of systematizing efforts, and the tendency to invoke its successes in order to obtain total victory. The following quotation is a reminder of the extremes to which these claims can go:

> The functions of barristers and solicitors could also be taken over. Lawyers face the problem of digesting masses of information, and here computers already have an enormous advantage over man. Ultimately, we are not only likely to have our case pleaded by computers but we shall be judged and sentenced by them. They are nothing if not impartial... Finally, if it were not only more rational but also very much more intelligent than a judge, the realisation would dawn that better justice could be dispensed by the unaided computer, and human judges would become redundant.[58]

The information or facts to be digested by the computer are dependent on the algorithm produced by the programmer or programmers. There may be areas of the law in which it is plausible to prevent the past, the facts of the case, from reaching the present and to point to the future. It is however hardly possible to predict the type of cases in which these attempts of rendering the fact-finding task purely retrodictive can be successful. The probability is high that in areas which are of the greatest concern to our times, above all in matters of technology assessments,

---

[56] *Cf., supra*, p. 24.
[57] Schopenhauer, for instance, distinguishes 40 of these forms, see *supra*, p. 83 n. 55, p. 32 ss.
[58] N.S. Sutherland, Professor of Experimental Psychology at the University of Sussex, "Revolution by Computer," *The Observer Review*, London, 9th April, 1967, p. 21.

one cannot treat the facts of the case as fossils of past events without falsifying their meanings.

Events are changes, and to adapt them to the capabilities of the computer requires formalizations which only a fully reliable tensed predicate logic could provide. This has not yet been achieved as the unresolved paradoxes of elementary logic cast their shadows over this branch of formal logic.

From the scientific point of view also, the claims of computer science appear to be without reliable foundation. It is difficult to accept as sheer coincidence that the disarray in which modern physics finds itself is contemporaneous with the borrowings it has made from the generalizations of algebra. Plato anticipated this by writing that only few mathematicians were able to reason right, implying that should they succeed, it would not be thanks to their knowledge of mathematics.[59]

Yet, some biologists hope or expect that "some day all biology will be reduced to physics and chemistry [which is] ideally, applied mathematics."[60] In this approach "wholes are explicable by analysis into their parts and events by their precedent events, which are their 'causes'."[61]

Technology hovers uneasily between contradictory positions. It clings to the principle of causality, which modern physics has discarded, yet it cannot ignore the theories of this science when it defends the validity of its decisions. In this dilemma, the preference of technology for megasolutions, notwithstanding the inability to control their consequences, indicates panic rather than planning. Science and technology had formed a common front against metaphysics. At the height of their triumphs a metaphysics "at the heart of rationalism"[62] was being discovered. This turned the model of rationality built before the downfall of causality into a house of cards. Computer technology has been the least affected by these developments. Relying on an outdated model of rationality it now presses for the conversion of jurisprudence into jurimetrics.[63]

We find support for this criticism in the last but one statement of the *Tractatus*:

My propositions serve as elucidations in the following way: Anyone who

---

[59] *Republic*, Bk. VII, 531E; and see Joseph Weizenbaum, *Computer Power and Human Reason* (San Francisco, 1976), p. 227.

[60] See Marjorie Grene, *The Knower and the Known* (London, 1966), p. 203.

[61] *Ibid.*

[62] Isaiah Berlin, *Four Essays on Liberty* (Oxford, 1969), p. 144, see also pp. 57 and 58, 79-80, 152-154.

[63] The distance which has been covered in a single decade may be gauged by a comparison of *Jurimetrics*, Hans W. Baade, ed. (New York, 1963), and Laurence H. Tride, *Channeling Technology Through Law* (Chicago, 1973).

understands me eventually recognizes them as nonsensical, when he has used them as steps to climb up beyond them. (He must, so to speak, throw away the ladder after he has climbed up it.) He must transcend these propositions and then he will see the world aright. (6.54)[64]

In an alternative predication one can say that it is the function of categories to deny themselves by showing how they can be transcended. In times of sweeping change this demonstration is not difficult to make.

It is instructive to compare this conclusion with that of Plato's *Republic*. This is not an attempt to assert that the *Tractatus* will have the enduring fame of the *Republic*, but that these works, starting from the opposite poles of logic and metaphysics, react to similar antinomies. Plato's work concludes with the expectation that, in following his advice to replace the present city of luxurious revel by his "Fair City," we may become "dear to ourselves and to the gods" forever and will "fare well."[65]

Wittgenstein sought to provide a spectacle for us, Plato our welfare. The former considered whether the mirror of a fully formalized logic could produce the right picture of the world. Plato holds out an end to alienation and with it the promise of happiness. In the *Tractatus* values are expelled into the beyond as their presence would distort the logical picture of the world. The expulsion is claimed to be justified as values are beyond language, they are ineffable. The salient distinction between the experience of the familiar and of the strange is here ignored. The boundaries between these two kinds of experience are blurred, and logic cannot operate unless these are clearcut, so that there will be no surprises even if this renders the grounds of a decision tautological. The overall result is an insensitivity to change and its dynamics as no effective logical calculus can be found for them. Plato's transcendental world in which the Form of Reason coincides with the Form of Being, is as impervious to change as Wittgenstein's logical world; both are resting immobile and immoveable in a beyond.

Their expositions have in common that they are made in parables or fables rather than being accounts of what there is.[66] In fables we welcome paradoxes, in factual statements they are suspect. By presenting us with the metaphor of the ladder Wittgenstein reinforces the shock which he prepared for us when at the end of a masterpiece he calls his elucidations "nonsensical." (6.541)

The options for the operations of teleological metaphysics are limited. They may renounce definitional control and their transcendental

---

[64] As C.L. Hamblin in his book, *Fallacies* (London, 1970), p. 95, pointed out, Wittgenstein must have received the metaphor of the ladder from Sextus Empiricus, *Against the Logicians II*, 480; see *Sexti Empirici Opera*, J.O. Fabricius, ed. (Leipzig, 1841), p. 553.

[65] Bks. X, 621 C and D and II, 372 E-373 B.

[66] See Plato, Laws 663d: Could there be a more useful fiction than that "an unjust life is... more truly unpleasant than a just and religious?"

thrust in order to remain on speaking terms with science. In this case the circularity of, for instance, the doctrine of "the survival of the fittest" will be acceptable. Again, it is being asserted that "the long-term welfare of human beings cannot be secured by policies that promote the interests of some people at the expense of others or even the interests of mankind at the expense of other living things."[67]

This implies that the welfare of human beings can be "secured," otherwise the proposition is implausible. One may criticize Platonic hypostases but the location of the "Fair City" above the heavens makes them immune against counterproof.

It is significant that according to the well-known biologists we have just quoted "expense" should be the standard of measurement. One is tempted to retort with Schopenhauer that life is a business which does not cover its costs, but the question is whether life is only a business. We shall revert to the notion of living on one's own resources and not at somebody else's expense.

The second option for metaphysics is to assert its priority over science. In this case a demonstration of autonomy is liable to lapse into orphic language of which the conclusion of *Parmenides,* a dialogue which discusses the problem of non-being, is an early, yet significant example.

> Further, let this be said: it seems that, whether there is or there is not a one, both that one and the others alike are and are not, and appear and do not appear to be, all manner of things in all manner of ways, with respect to themselves and to one another. Very true.[68]

These lines are a fitting finale to Plato's attempt to find a logical solution to the perennial problem of negation.[69] This is of special interest in reference to the procedural rules on denials. The failure of Plato and his epigones — in the sense in which all philosophers in the West are in part at least his epigones — to find a "rational" solution of the problem of negation places a restraint on the urge to set up rigorous rules of pleadings. As recent reforms[70] show, the law is becoming increasingly aware of the need for this restraint.

A further option is to remain silent. This recommendation forms the conclusion of the *Tractatus.* We are glad that Wittgenstein had not followed his own advice entirely.

---

[67] Peter and Jean Medawar, *The Life Science* (London, 1977), p. 173.
[68] In the translation by F.M. Cornford in *The Collected Dialogues of Plato,* Edith Hamilton and Huntington Cairns, eds. (Princeton, 1973), p. 956, whose version achieves greater lucidity than a more literal treatment of the text.
[69] See David Wiggins, "Sentence Meaning, Negation and Plato's Problem of Non-Being" in *Plato, A Collection of Critical Essays,* Gregory Vlastos, ed. (Garden City, N.Y.), Vol. I, pp. 298-302 and *cf., supra,* pp. 32-35.
[70] See *supra,* p. 76.

SHIFTING THE BURDEN OF PROOF

The need to test matters of technology and science in the ordinary courts frequently arises in actions for negligence and nuisance. In these, a typical issue of fact is the escape or emission of allegedly harmful substances, and the plaintiff may belong to an indeterminate class of claimants. Claims of this type are gaining a new importance as the risks which the defendant faces may be uninsurable or prohibitively expensive to insure. In this type of litigation the need for the opinion of a court-appointed expert may be acute.

In these cases there will be an imbalance between the form of the expert evidence and the structure of the substantive norm. The opinion will refer to systematizations which offer themselves for conceptual analysis. This evidence will be directed towards torts which escape definition, are described in circularities and dispense with clearcut boundaries as guaranty of their normative integrity.[71] These torts are situation bound and reflect a history of sociality and fundamental convictions. The experience of this history is being challenged by each important new technology or scientific hypothesis when they become relevant in a proceedings.

In order to show adjudicative means of overcoming inherent tensions between fact and value in the fact-finding task it is however not necessary to consider the most recent or the most esoteric developments. In *Cook v. Lewis*[72] two parties hunting grouse were close to each other when two members of one party fired at different birds and in different directions. As a result, a member of the other party was injured by one shot. The actors fired knowing that the injured party was in the vicinity or without making sure that he was not in the line of fire. The majority in the Supreme Court of Canada confirmed the judgment in the Court of Appeal of British Columbia. This judgment held in effect that both actors were liable even if it could not be determined which of the two had fired the shot in question. The majority in the Supreme Court of Canada found it irrelevant to determine whether the two actors were in a sufficiently close association to be liable as "joint tortfeasors,"[73] an "operational" concept. The relevant elements of the situation were the behaviour of the two actors upon the presence of the two parties in the same vicinity. In the particular circumstances of this encounter it was impossible to attribute the shot in question to one actor to the exclusion of the other. This impossibility led the majority to find a shift in the burden of proof from the injured party which imposed on each of the actors the burden to prove their denials. It will be noted that by this

---

[71] For the vagueness of the legal concept of nuisance see Cecil A. Wright, *Cases in the Law of Torts*, 2nd ed. (Toronto, 1958), p. 676.

[72] [1951] S.C.R. 830 at pp. 835 and 842.

[73] *I.e.*, persons who together commit a civil, as opposed to a criminal wrong.

shift an issue of causality became irrelevant. The reason for the shift was made explicit by Cartwright, J. He relied on a decision in a court in the United States of America where it was held:

> The injured party had been placed by defendants in the unfair position of pointing to which defendant caused the harm.

The decision of the Supreme Court of Canada has far-reaching implications for situations in which there is a substantial pre-existing potentiality of harm. Typically, modern processing methods involve the use of high energy and temperatures in chemical rather than mechanical processes. These methods vastly increase the probability and range of harm. This change in processing methods increases also the difficulty of finding a reliable calculus capable of linking a given situation to an impugned behaviour. Hence, where the issue of a shift in the burden of proof arises, there will often be the difficulty of determining the extent of this shift. On this specific point alone, the opinion of a court-appointed expert can make a considerable contribution to the fact-finding task.

This contribution will be of particular importance when the shift of the burden of proof is being ordered on an appeal and the technological or scientific issues involved are new or complex. Issues of this kind will come before the courts with increasing frequency. In appeal cases, several members of the court, while agreeing on the end result, regularly hand down separate reasons for judgments. The differences between them may affect the determination of the extent of the shift in the burden of proof. There may arise also the further difficulty that the actual determination of this extent will not be made by the appeal court itself but left to the lower court to which the case is referred for re-consideration or a new trial. This court may have to take into account the tenor of the several judgments of the majority in the court of appeal.

It may be of interest on this point that in the view of the civil law the practice of handing down separate judgments appears to border on the irrational. In many civil law jurisdictions the court hands down not only a single decision but it also speaks with a single voice as to the reasons for judgment. Neither dissents nor differences regarding the reasons for judgment are made public. To a lawyer in a common jurisdiction this practice seems to owe much to the persistent splendour of the systematizations which had been achieved in the great codes of the civil law. It is often forgotten that the fact content of a provision in a code had originally been taken from a precedent which in turn depended on the relevances determined in the fact-finding task of a concrete case.

The asystemic character of the law of negligence and nuisance makes this civil law practice inapplicable in the common law. The case *Cook v.*

Lewis[74] itself makes this apparent. The shift in the burden of proof was made on grounds of fairness, a term that is not definable and difficult to translate. By the appeal to fairness the facts are made the servants of value.[75] The imperfections of servants are more easily forgiven than those of masters. And yet, experience shows how fatal the risks are of ignoring on a journey to the "Fair City" above the heavens the facticity of the human world.

However, the desire itself to reach this destination or a nostalgia to return to it is a consequence of the experience of this facticity. Logic may point to the gap between fact and value, to their separation by structural incompatibilities, but the law can fill this gap as one of its functions, perhaps even the most important one, is to mediate between fact and value.

To elucidate this function, we shall turn to poetry whose equivocations provide at times, and especially in times of sweeping change, better insights than the constructs of philosophy. In describing the relation of the Greek citizen to his city-state, we quoted from a chorus in Sophocles' *Antigone*.[76] The plot of this tragedy illustrates the problematics of theories of natural justice. The opening lines of this chorus set the theme:

> There are many strange things in the world but nothing is stranger than man;"[77]

Then follows a description of man's technical achievements, his cleverness and skills. At the close there is a reference to human law:

> he treads a path between the laws of the earth and the oathbound justice of the gods;[78]

The earth was described as "ageless and untiring," hence homologous to the permanence of divine justice. In this way achievable balances and mediating harmonies between the things and behaviour towards them are being projected. So, Sophocles in his pious serenity. His contemporary Aeschylus, more conservative and more profound, described these relations in a sombre mood. In two lines, which allegorize monstrous crimes committed by members of a royal house against each other, he speaks of the eagles "who sacrifice a poor trembling (hare) with all her unborn young."[79] At one level he invokes

---

[74] See *supra* n. 72.
[75] See *supra* pp. 13 and 72.
[76] *Supra* p. 43 n. 2.
[77] *Ibid.* line 332; the adjective "strange" corresponds best to the meanings of the original expression which runs the gamut from "terrifying," "mighty," "strange" and "cunning" to "skillful."
[78] *Ibid.*, 369.
[79] *Agamemnon*, 137-8; for the hybris in wantonly plundering a bird's nest see *ibid.* 49-54.

compassion and horror but at another there is the implication that beings behave "rationally"[80] and in accordance with the laws of the earth, even "altruistically" as with their prey they feed their own young. Inherent limitations of justice and its internal conflicts are indicated here.

Aeschylus agrees with Sophocles' premise of man's terrifying, forceful strangeness but does not follow him into a possible reconciliation of fundamental polarities. Instead, Aeschylus traced the line along which hunger for power emancipates itself from its physical counterpart.

These ancient writings show unsolved fundamental problems which have accompanied and pre-occupied man throughout the intervening millenia. They suggest that the utmost vigilance, careful initiative and self-restraint are needed if stabilizing immunities are to be protected. As long as they remain intact, the fact-finding task of the law can afford to ignore the history of the sacrifices which make existing social balances possible.

It is different in times of sweeping change in which new technologies play their part in opening up new perspectives. Their meanings for the law can be discovered only if fact finding is sufficiently equipped for its task. The starting line for its adjustment to the actualities of the times is located in the strategically decisive fields of procedure and evidence. If the rule-changes which have been made in this regard are not being put to use, justice will find itself blinded when on encountering the strange it removes its blindfold.

THE ADVERSARY PRINCIPLE

Before reaching the close of these inquiries, we shall revert once more to the *Phillips* case;[81] it was decided in a jurisdiction where the rules made no provision for court-appointed expert witnesses. However, even where a new rule to this effect was introduced,[82] it has hardly ever been used. It is difficult to accept that there have been no important cases since, in which a conflict of expert opinion on technological issues could not have been resolved by the opinion of a court-appointed expert. Without it the only means for the disposition of the case will often be a decision according to the distribution of the burden of proof. As the taking of risks is inherent in the use of a new technology, a decision that fails to come to grips with the facts in issue due to the stalemate created by an opinion-conflict is a second-rate decision. And to shift

---

[80] *I.e.*, according to the "maximin" calculus, see *supra* p. 53, n. 23.
[81] See *Phillips v. Ford Motor Co., supra,* n. 44.
[82] *Supra*, p. 76.

responsibility for the decision to administrative bodies with their special interests amounts to a renunciation of judicial responsibility.

The deeper reason for the unconditional application of the adversary principle,[83] which the absence of a court-appointed witness signifies, deserves further attention. Courts of justice are to dispense justice, and the rules of procedure and evidence are designed to this purpose. The semantic field of the term "justice" reaches from cosmology to morality. In a larger perspective it is the constitutive and regulative principle which presides over nature as a whole inclusive of persons and groups. In consequence "he who does not justly perform his appointed task, may appear as a violator of the whole order of the universe."[84] Projections of this view are still with us to-day.[85]

In a narrower view justice is administered by persons to persons, holds or does not hold between them and addresses itself only to them. The cosmological conception of justice is laid aside. There, myth shows Themis, the goddess of law and order, counselling Zeus on the eternal laws and her daughters Justice (Dike), Law-abidingness and Peace, the latter with the infant Wealth, to administer the laws below. The myth proclaims the hierarchical relation between the eternal laws of nature and human laws.[86] Fundamental problems of fact finding are thus bypassed.

The transcendental view of justice, in which eternal laws validate and illuminate human laws, bears on the perennial "either/or" question whether the situation giving rise to litigation is attributable to a decree of destiny or to a refusal to follow the way of the law. Western civilization embraced the latter alternative; it became its predominant characteristic. The antipole is the determinism of Darwinism and of historical materialism; both have lost ground in the West.[87] A juxtaposition of the Icelandic *Njal's Saga*[88] with Aeschylus' *Eumenides* will illustrate early conceptions of the alternatives. Being early, they are unburdened by subsequent adumbrations and variations. Both works show the development of an administration of justice as an

---

[83] *Supra*, p. vii; for a survey and evaluation of this principle see Neil Brooks, *The Judge and the Adversary System*, Osgoode Hall Annual Lecture Series 1976, Allan M. Linden, ed., Downsview, p. 89.

[84] Quoted by F.M. Cornford, *From Religion to Philosophy* (New York, 1957), p. 54, in a presentation of this view and its implications; the apothegm is attributed to Pythagoras.

[85] For the historial ebb and flow of governing themes in cosmology and their reoccurrences in modern physics see R.G. Collingwood, *The Idea of Nature* (Oxford, 1964), esp. pp. 143-157 and 169-170.

[86] *Cf., supra*, p. 90.

[87] *On the Origin of Species* and the original version of the first chapter of *Das Kapital* were both published in 1859.

[88] *Njal's Saga*, tr., intr. and annot. by Carl F. Bayerschmidt and Lee M. Hollander (New York, 1955).

institution of the state. Insofar as the Saga is an authentic relation of the period it describes and not a posthumous interpretation, the background is that of a shame-, not a guilt-culture, and everything turns on innate character, this is to say destiny.[89] In contrast, in the *Eumenides* the emphasis is on guilt as consequence of personal responsibility. Innate character does not make a contribution to the plot. Law, as it emerged in ancient Greece as well as in Judaea, demands in order to realize itself an overall commitment; its firmness depends on character-building, this is to say on an act of self-determination. The self-determination of the person is seen to promote the integration of the group. Here are the grounds for the loyalty which the adversary principle inspires. Adherence to it is not only a matter of sound practice, it proclaims the tenet that in his encounters with others and with nature civilized man is a self-determining being. The development of this doctrine has been too often described to require recapitulation. The ancient Germanic people however considered their gods to be without immortality, and inscrutable destiny to stand paramount in a world which was as mortal as its gods.[90] This belief obstructed a world-view, in which law and ethics had a transcendental, common origin. Yet those who discern traces of the resistance of the common law to legal transcendentalism, for instance in its tardy acceptance of the civil law doctrine of contributary negligence, may be reminded that in the 16th century a bill of indictment for a felony described at times the offence as being "contrary to the Common Law and the Ten Commandments."

The tenet of self-determination manifests itself in the agonistic form of a law suit. However, this characteristic is realized fully only in issues which are being adjudicated under the substantive rules of the common law and the statutes derived from it. It is different if the case turns on a rule of Equity, the "higher" law, where the decree is often granted on terms which mediate the claims of the parties. This function will determine the parameter and relevances of the fact-finding task.[91] The question here is whether, regardless of the kind of substantive law involved, in matters of technology assessments, especially in those which are explained in terms of complex or advanced scientific theories, the polythetic, topical mode of fact finding is preferable to the logico-systematic mode which results in the presentation of atomic facts.

---

[89] For the emphasis on character see *ibid.* ss. 42-44.
[90] *Cf.*, Lars Loennroth, *Njals Saga, A Critical Introduction* (California U.P., 1976), p. 58: "Fate, however, is often represented as an impersonal force working behind the visible scene of action . . . . . beyond is nothing before the arrival of the Christian God." In the law a related issue comes to the fore in the polarities of crime- and criminal-oriented administration of justice.
[91] *Cf.*, George H. Kendal, "The Role of Concepts in the Legal Process" (1962), 1 *U.B.C.L.R.* 617 at pp. 640-1.

For this we shall draw together the several conclusions of our earlier descriptions. They do not claim to show an isomorphic conformity; there are however sufficient affinities to indicate the cumulative support they provide for each other. We began our inquiries by showing the basic elements of matter to be hypothetically conceived and not perceived. Yet, fact-finding is concerned with perceivable things, and percepts do not show one thing to the exclusion of others but some in a stronger and others in a weaker light. This, however, does not turn the differences in the appearance of things into uncircuitous polarities. These serve both as justification and as aim of the "either/or" mode of fact-description. In justification they presuppose a dualistic world-view to which a particular fact-finding task seeks to conform for its validity. However, the axis which defines the poles masks the feasibility of reaching one pole from the other in either direction. Moreover, as a point, a pole is without dimensions so that strictly speaking one cannot reach, only circumnavigate it. If so, a pole is a mark or sign-post rather than a terminus. Further, the act of perceiving does not take place within the matrix of dualistic Cartesian coordinates but within a perspective which encompasses the triad of figure, ground and horizon so that the "either/or" mode of determination will not serve as universal model. Again, in remembering, which in fact finding is always a matter of concern, it is not a case of "either I remember or I don't" but of an indeterminable selectivity so that, except perhaps in the most drastic instances, an event is and is not remembered.

In fact finding, it is not a question of whether a thing is or is not but except in familiar, simple cases a matter of probability assessments. And the facts which are relevant to the assessment of advanced technologies are neither familiar nor simple. Further, at least in the concrete case, degrees of probability are not quantitatively determinable so that the boundaries between them are blurred — unless one is willing to grant to mathematical logic more outward powers than it can justify. That we tolerate a mode of fact finding which leads to atomic descriptions means that familiarity with a given situation encourages us to take short-cuts. Technology assessments in litigation will deal however frequently with the new, the unfamiliar. Moreover, a new technology changes not only the technical product and the ground on which it is being made or used but also the horizon of these behaviours.

In descriptions on causal lines each singular link of the projected chain can be tested without regard to the remainder, as the test has an absolute "either/or" structure. As we have seen this is not the case when the polythetic, topical approach is being used. In assessments of complex and advanced technology this approach can be ignored only at the risk of falsifying the result. There is a growing conviction that the logical paradoxes are neither toys invented for our amusement nor insignificant exceptions but that they are symptoms of an insufficiency at the heart of logic and therefore of the logico-systematic form of reasoning in fact finding. Gödel's theorem has shown the inherent limitations of system-building by means of the axiomatic method[92] common to both mathematics and logic. The preference for "either/or" solutions, which this method produces, rests on the assumptions that the law of the excluded middle[93] is the law of reason, and that this reason is the law of the world.

This is not to say that in familiar situations the short-cuts which "either/or" decision structures permit, should be avoided and with them the adversary mode of fact finding, provided one remembers that what is being done is the taking of short-cuts with the accompanying risk that relevant sign-posts will be missed, but the greater the change, the greater this risk. Only in stagnant societies can technological behaviour be unchanging behaviour. In the "post-industrial" age we are no longer at the stage of modifying and maximizing existing techniques but in times when new ground in the field of technology is being broken. At this stage, we can no longer stay content with the simplifications and short-cuts of the "either/or" mode of reasoning. However, the prestige of this mode has survived, and one cannot expect experts to forego of a sudden the traditional manner of delivering their opinions. However, a third opinion can counteract the stultifying stalemates which the clash of opinion allows. A court-appointed expert can act as critic, and technology assessments stand in need of disinterested criticality.

The adversary principle is the governing theme of legal procedure. The procedural steps are specified and they are limited in number. To this extent procedure is systematized. However, some procedural decisions are in the discretion of a party, some in the combined discretion of the parties and the judge and others again are in his exclusive discretion. The interplay of these powers may be observed even in a simple application for an adjournment. Rules of procedure are rules of practice, and in practice discretionary rules can be as important as the mandatory rules. The conditions, in which discretionary powers can be properly exercised, challenge the overall systemic character of procedure.

Pythagoras believed that he knew "the whole order of universe," and others since have hoped that all that is "as yet" unknown shall soon or eventually become known. We cannot share these hopes with any degree of confidence. The alternative is to satisfy the desire for certainties by treating a scientific concept as a reification of reason, and the reification as a scientific fact. However, the hypothetical character of scientific theory creates here a dilemma. It would be otherwise if

---

[92] See Nagel and Newman *Gödel's Proof* (New York, 1964), pp. 59-60, n. 13.
[93] *Supra*, p. 73.

these theories, as they follow each other in history, are progressive approximations to an ideal of absolute, as opposed to statistical validity. This assumption leads farther down the path of Platonism than Plato himself may have wished to go in setting up polarities and then trying to synthesize them. Had he taken the transcendental Forms or Ideas of his *Republic* at their face value, he would not have considered it necessary to write later on his *Laws,* a work which owes nothing to his theory of Forms. Reference is made here to these ancient endeavours of giving meaning to the human world so that any distance we have moved since may be gauged better.

To do so without pre-judgments, it was necessary to range far in diachronic and synchronic directions. Only in this way could a frame of reference be obtained for the many-layered web of problems of fact finding. This perspective yielded points of resemblance between the several initial descriptions and the configuration of the fact-finding task. Unless the resemblances are being dismissed as coincidental, they are a confirmation of the faithfulness of the descriptions. One of their consequences is that the exception to the adversary principle, which the calling of an expert witness by the court signifies, is not a sacrilege. Moving now towards the close of these inquiries we may well ponder on a question which Sophocles asked. It forms the conclusion of a description of the limits in which natural forces operate: "And we, when shall we learn moderation?"[94]

---

[94] Ajax, 677; the maxim *Fiat justitia, ruat coelum* presents a different exhortation; for the epistemological significance of the virtue of moderation (Sophrosyne) and the dilemmas to which it leads in Idealism see Stanley Rosen, "Sophrosyne and Selbstbewusstsein" (1972/3), 26 *Review of Metaphysics* 617.

Chapter 6

A Conclusion

In matters concerning the procurement of goods needed for the well being of the singular person and his or her dependants, there is an accumulated stock of lived experience which has made the patterns of the legal transaction involved fully familiar. In a sale-of-goods statute the reference to "the intention of the parties" is common to many important provisions. Often, this reference is being interpreted as a *ceteris paribus* proviso[1] and leads to a finding of a putative intention. One would therefore expect the reference to widen significantly the parameter of relevant facts. However, as the pattern of transactions, from offer to delivery or transfer of title, are familiar, the operating concepts which describe the behaviour involved can be accepted as a sufficient framework for allegations of fact and denials in the majority of the transactions which result in litigation. If disputes over these transactions arise that do not involve the problematics of new technologies or of state intervention, it would be an exercise in futility to replace the logico-systematic method of determining relevances and facts with the topical approach. Hence, in litigation of this type the traditional rules of procedure and evidence may be applied with confidence.

It is different in cases where new technologies or matters of public policy are making a direct impact on modes of production and concomitant social conditions. In these cases, which frequently concern a technological megasolution, the logico-systematic method should be applied with caution and the topical approach be utilized to keep a check on the relevance and plausibility of allegations of fact and their denials as well as on the evidence which is being adduced. For this, the rules of procedure and evidence need flexibility so as to give the topical approach its full opportunity in the fact-finding task. It will not be possible to keep these two ways completely distinct in all cases and there will be clashes of incompatibility between them. However, these conflicts over the instrumentalities of a fact-finding task need not lead to a stultification of the legal process if Bench and Bar alike remain alert to the possibilities of compromise solutions.

The advantages of the logico-systematic method can best be seen in taxation law. It is the most thoroughly conceptualized branch of the law,

---

[1] This qualification indicates that a rule be applied only if the transaction in issue closely resembles the model contemplated by the rule.

and its operating concepts and definitions are directed throughout towards the full utilization of method. Hence, an automated, computerized system of accounting is capable of making income tax returns, this is to say provisional decisions on tax liability, in the same process in which the facts in the case, the profit and loss statements and balance sheets are being produced. Moreover, the computer is capable of acting as critic of the accounting system in use by ringing the changes on a series of alternative systems in order to determine which of them could produce the most favourable result.

At the other end of the spectrum are many, if not most areas of domestic relations where the topical approach is needed to reach the value judgments by which problems of domestic relations are being resolved. It is significant that in the concrete case the relations involved and their legal consequences may change their character with the speed of lightning so that many of the solutions can be provisional only. They will accordingly carry the proviso: "Liberty to apply." It may be worth noting that, under the influence of Rationalism, family law tried to quantify the types and degrees of "domestic offences" by establishing for them a point system which determined the outcome of the litigation. The absurdity of these attempts at systematization was eventually noticed in modern family law where a topical approach is now being taken. There will, however, be cases in which method points to a certain clearcut decision and the topical approach to a solution of a kind which would be incompatible with that decision. To these cases of confrontation applies the observation of Holmes that "great cases make bad law." It is impossible to retrodict how much of this failure is due to the neglect of the topical approach at the fact-finding stage. Not only would one need a transcript of the entire proceedings but also the preparatory material of each party in order to see whether some sources of evidence had not been rejected in advance according to an exclusive interpretation of the fact-content seemingly stipulated by the norm.

Regarding technology assessments made in the ordinary courts it is significant that time and time again opposing social ideologies have been univocal in approving the megasolutions which typically a quantity-oriented research recommends. It is one of the many examples of extremes touching each other. Characteristically, many accommodations between these ideologies are being achieved at the level of this contact, the qualitative issues being dismissed with an unconvincing shrug of regret. In times of sweeping change, however, these issues will leap over the domain of social ideology into that of cosmology where archaelogical layers of experience which interpenetrate each other will often be found. The topical approach to the fact-finding task offers a viable alternative. This approach cannot tolerate the self-imposed censorship of restrictive practices in matters of procedure and evidence, of which the exclusion of the court-appointed expert is the most important example. To continue with these practices means the further erosion of the authority of the fact-finding and other decision-making processes.

Appendix A

Gorgias: On What is Not or on Nature*

Though, at the outset, Gorgias of Leontini took the same position as those who demolish the criterion, his line of attack was different from that of Protagoras. In his *On What is Not or on Nature* he consecutively advanced three main points: First and foremost that nothing *is*; second that even if something *is*, man cannot apprehend it; and third that even if it was apprehensible, it surely cannot be elucidated and communicated to the next man. (66) The conclusion that nothing *is* was reached by him in the following way: If something *is*, it either *is* or not or it both *is* and *is* not. But he will establish that being neither *is* nor, so he will assure, nonbeing nor, as he will impart also, both being and nonbeing. Hence it is not so that something *is* (67) and, above all, nonbeing *is* not.

For if nonbeing *is*, it will at one and the same time be and not be; for in so far as it is conceived as nonbeing, it will not be; on the other hand, in so far as it *is* nonbeing, it will again be. But it would be quite absurd for something to be and at the same time not to be. Nonbeing indeed *is* not. Moreover, in case nonbeing *is*, being will not be. They are paired as part and counterpart, and if being thus appertains to nonbeing, nonbeing will appertain to being. It is not so that being *is* not. Hence nonbeing will not be. (68) And yet being *is* not. For if it *is*, it is either sempiternal or brought forth or both sempiternal and brought forth. But, as we shall show, being is neither sempiternal nor brought forth nor both; being therefore *is* not. For if it is sempiternal (one has to start with this), it is without origin.

(69) For everything brought forth has an origin but the sempiternal, not being brought forth, is without origin; and not having an origin, it is undifferentiated, impenetrable and boundless. If it is so, it is nowhere for if it is anywhere that, in which it is, is something other than it. It would then be surrounded by something and therefore no longer be boundless. For that which surrounds something is larger than that which is being surrounded but nothing is larger than the boundless;

---

* One of the summaries of this lost work which has survived is that by Sextus Empiricus (adv. math. VII 65-87). The version by Sextus Empiricus is considered superior, and this translation is based on the emended text in *Die Fragmente der Vorsokratiker*, Hermann Diels ed., 11th ed. (Zuerich, 1964), Vol. II, B3, pp. 279-283. This translation has profited greatly from those by R.D. Bury, *Sextus Empiricus* (London & Cambridge, Mass., 1955), Vol. II, pp. 35-45 and by George Kennedy in *The Older Sophists*, Rosamond Kent Sprague ed. (U. of S. Carolina Press, 1972), pp. 42-46.

hence the boundless is nowhere. (70) It surely cannot surround itself by itself, for then that wherein it is and that which is therein will be the same, and being will become two things, place and body, place as that wherein it is and body as that which is therein. But this is absurd. In itself, therefore, being *is* not. So that if being is sempiternal it is undifferentiated, impenetrable and boundless; if so, it is nowhere, and if it is nowhere it *is* not. Accordingly, if being is sempiternal, it *is* not in any way. (71) Surely, being cannot be something which was brought forth. For this to be so, being would have to be brought forth either out of being or of nonbeing. But it was not brought forth out of being, for if it *is*, it was not brought forth but was always already there and it was not brought forth out of nonbeing, for nonbeing cannot bring forth anything; to do so, nonbeing would necessarily have to partake of some generative power. Surely, being was therefore not brought forth. (72) These considerations apply also to a joinder of the sempiternal and what was brought forth. They cancel each other out, and if being is sempiternal, it was not brought forth, and if it was brought forth, it is not sempiternal. Hence, if being is neither sempiternal nor brought forth nor the joinder of both, it cannot be. (73) Again, if it *is*, it is either a single entity or a plurality, but, as will be shown, being is neither the one nor the other, hence being *is* not. For if it is a single entity, it would have quantity, cohesion, area or volume. But whichever of these it be, being is not a single entity, as quantity allows for division and cohesion can be severed; likewise a single entity, conceived as area, will not be indivisible, and as for volume, there are three dimensions, length, width and depth. It would be absurd to say that being has none of them, hence being is not a single entity. (74) Yet neither is it a plurality. For if it is not a single entity, it is not a plurality either. The latter is a combination of singular units, wherefore, once the feasibility of a single entity is refuted, that of plurality falls with it. Since clearly neither being nor nonbeing *are*, (75) it can also now readily be concluded that the conjunction of being and nonbeing *is* not. For if being and nonbeing together *are*, nonbeing would in regard to being be one and the same, and for this reason neither of them *is*. For it is agreed that nonbeing *is* not; further it has been shown that being is one and the same as nonbeing; accordingly it also will not be. (76) In any case, if being is one and the same as nonbeing, both of them cannot be; for if both are, they cannot be one and the same, and if they are one and the same, there are not two. From this it follows that nothing *is*. For if neither being nor nonbeing *is* nor both, and as in this regard nothing else is conceivable, nothing *is*.

(77) Next, it has to be shown that, even if anything *is*, man cannot know or conceive it. For, as Gorgias expresses it, if thoughts are not beings, being is not thought. The following analogy holds: Just as, if things which are thought can be white and therefore white things can be

thought, so, if things, which *are* not, can be thought, then necessarily things which *are* might not be thought. (78) For this reason, the following is sound and helpful in its consequentiality: "If the things thought are not beings, being is not thought." Thoughts are not beings (one has to start with this), and so shall we show; being is indeed not thought, and, plainly, thoughts are not beings. (79) For if thoughts are beings, all thoughts are so, in any way someone may think them. This is however nonsense (if it was so, it would be a sorry state of affairs). It is not so that, if one thinks of a man as flying or of chariots running on the sea, forthwith he is flying or chariots are running on the sea. Hence thoughts are not beings. (80) Besides, if thoughts are beings, things which *are* not could not be thought. Part and counterpart belong together, and nonbeing is the counterpart of being. It follows that, if thinking and being thus belong together, nonthinking and nonbeing also belong together. But this is absurd, for Scylla and the Chimaera as well as many other nonbeings are thought. Being is indeed not thought. (81) Just as on account of its visibility what is being seen is stated to be seen and what is being heard is on account of its audibility stated to be heard, and we do not reject what is visible because it is not heard nor dismiss what is audible because it is not seen (for each should be judged according to the faculty of the sense involved and not of another), so it is with thoughts, even if they should not be viewed by the sight or heard by the hearing, as thoughts are grasped according to the criteria of judgment appropriate to them. (82) If then a man thinks of chariots running on the sea, he ought to believe that there are chariots running on the sea, even if he does not observe it. This would however be absurd; therefore being is not thought and it is not apprehended.

(83) And even if being is apprehensible, it cannot be brought to light for another. For if beings are visible and audible and thus objects of common perception, this is to say they belong to the external world, where visible things are apprehensible by the act of seeing and audible things by the act of hearing and not conversely, how can they then be communicated to another? (84) By language, which is indeed the means of making something known, but words are not subsisting beings. We do indeed not impart to our neighbours the things which are, but words, and they are different from the things which subsist. Accordingly, just as the visible will not become the audible or conversely, so since being subsists externally, it will not become our language, (85) and not being language, it will not be revealed to another. Moreover, he asserts, speech conjoins the external events which impact on us, this is those events which are perceptible by the senses. For when we meet with a certain flavour, there is produced for us language so as to describe its quality, and, by the impact of a colour, language regarding its colour. If so, it is not speech that animates the external world, but speech makes it possible to inform ourselves about it. (86) One certainly cannot assert

that speech subsists in the manner of visible and audible things so that speech by its subsistence and being can reveal the things as they subsist and are. For, so he says, even if speech subsists, it is a mode of subsistence unlike that of other things, there being a great difference between visible bodies and speech. A different organ is involved in apprehending the visible and comprehending speech. Therefore, speech does not manifest the manifold of subsisting things, just as these do not disclose themselves to each other.

(87) These are the problems raised by Gorgias so that in the result the criterion of truth has disappeared. For there cannot be a criterion of that which neither *is* nor can be known and which, by its nature, is incommunicable to another.

Index

Aeschylus, 90-91
Allegations and denials of facts, 72-74
Argument on facts, 81
Atomic theory in antiquity, 26

Being and Becoming, 34, 40-41, 102
Belief, 13, 28n, 36
Boykowych v. Boykowych, 61

Carneades, 19-21
Causality
   Burden of Proof, 88-89
   Cause/effect concatenation, 27, 77-78
   Ontology, 28
Cicero, 20, 63-64
Cook v. Lewis, 88-89
Cosmology, 47, 61, 63-64, 92

Decision-making models, 54
Describing
   Change, 2, 71, 73
   Metaphor, 2
   Redundancy, 18
   Systematization, 28, 63; *see also* Systematic order
   Topical, 12, 27-28
Diagrammatic representation, 46-48
Diaz v. Gonzales, 61

Equity, 67, 93
Etherealization
   Language, 13, 70
   Law, 44
   Nature, 1, 37
   Technology, 10

Experience, 3-5
Expert evidence, 78-79, 81-82, 83

Fact-finding, adjudicative, 77-78, 88, 94
Fallacies, 19, 83
Familiarity, 10, 12, 22, 24

Gödel's Theorem of Incompleteness, 37, 38, 57-58, 95
Gorgias, 33-34, 35-36, 101-104
Group personality and structure, 45-48

Heisenberg's Indeterminacy Principle, 25-26, 68
Heraclitus
   Harmony, 40
   Strife, 26

Interventionist State, 51

Laws
   Justiciary, 49-50, 68, 90-92, 95
   Nature, 61, 73, 77, 90
Logic
   Axioms, 31, 58
   Computer
      Operations, 55-56
      Subroutines, 59-60
   Elementary, 56-57
   Formal, 39-40
   Language, 13, 62-63, 70-71
   Laws
      Excluded middle, 73, 95
      Non-contradiction, 33, 38
   Many-valued, 67-68

Logic—*continued*
　Paradoxes
　　Negation, 1, 31, 34, 101-102
　　Non-existence, 33-34
　　Self-reflexive, 72n, 94-95
　　Particle theory, 1, 38
　　Propositional, 39, 72, 73-74
　　Tautology, 32-33, 72, 86
　　Value, 13, 71, 86

Maximization, 9, 64, 98

Negation
　Entailment, 39
　General conceptions, 32, 73-74
　Infinite regress, 32-33

Perceptual structures, 2-5
Phillips v. Ford Motor Co., 78, 80-81, 91
Plato
　Literacy, 4
　Mathematicians, 85
　Ontology, 69, 87
　Theories
　　Forms, 34, 69, 96
　　Negation, 34-35
Pleadings
　Causality, 79
　History, 65-66
　Logical implication, 75
Possibility, 18-19
Probability
　Behaviour, 20, 21
　Relevance, 24-25
　Stoic conception, 23
　Theories, 19

Quantification, 17, 18, 27, 71, 85

Rationality
　Law of reason, 95
　Polarity, 67, 94

Rationality—*continued*
　Rational actor, 54-55
　Reasonableness, 52-53
　Subsumption, 74
　Systematization, 9, 19, 28, 50; see also Systematic order
Recollection
　Historicity, 6
　Seriation, 5

Scientific knowledge
　General, 37-38
　Specialization, 24, 78
　Theory, 37-38
Self-determination, 6, 93
Sociality, 7, 43-44, 45, 47
Solipsism, 5
Sophocles, 43n, 90-91, 96
Systematic order
　Change, 13-14, 15
　Normative, 50, 66, 89-90, 95
　Technology, 9-10

Topics
　Cumulation, 24, 27-28, 71-72, 77-78
　Problem-solving, 67, 72
Transactional directness, 48-50
Triadic patterns, vii, 67-68

Uncertainty, 5, 12-13, 25-26, 52-53, 55, 67; see also Gödel's Theorem of Incompleteness and Heisenberg's Indeterminacy Principle

Value judgment, 61, 67, 72, 74
Visual bias, 3-4

Wittgenstein
　Causality, 28n
　Facts, 71-73
　Negation, 31

AUG 2 2 1983 **DATE DUE**

8/2/86

GAYLORD PRINTED IN U.S.A.